Evaluation in Adult and Further Education: A Practical Handbook for Teachers and Organisers

J05

JUDITH EDWARDS

The Workers' Educational Association
West Lancashire and Cheshire District

Published in 1991 by The Workers' Educational Association,
7/8 Bluecoat Chambers, School Lane, Liverpool, L1 3BX.

Copyright Judith Edwards, 1991
ISBN 0 948374 02 0

Cover Design: Julie Hollis
Cartoons: Ian Hering

Printed in England by
Printfine Limited, Gibraltar Row,
King Edward Industrial Estate, Liverpool

In the beginning God created the heaven and the earth . . .
And God saw everything that He made
"Behold," God said, "it is very good."
And the evening and the morning were the sixth day

And on the seventh day God rested from all his work.
His archangel came then unto Him asking:
"God, how do you know that what you have created is
'very good'?
What are your criteria? On what data do you base your
judgement? Aren't you a little close to the situation to make
a fair and unbiased evaluation?"

God thought about these questions all that day and
His rest was greatly disturbed.
On the eighth day God said, "Lucifer, go to hell."

Thus was evaluation born in a blaze of glory.

From *Halcolm's*
The Real Story of Paradise Lost

Quoted in **M. Q. Patton (1981) Creative Evaluation.**

Contents

Acknowledgements

In preparing and writing this book I am indebted to the many students who have participated in evaluation exercises and from whom I have learned so much; and to colleagues, family and friends who have contributed ideas and given support. Elizabeth Whale especially, has generously shared her ideas and materials and offered encouragement over many years. Many thanks also go to Ian Hering of City College, Liverpool, for the cartoons, Julie Hollis (student of the BTEC National Diploma in Graphic Design, City College) for the cover design and to David Connor, formerly District Secretary of the Workers' Educational Association, West Lancashire and Cheshire District.

Finally, thank you Paul, Sophie and Tom for your patient helpfulness and good humour!

Introduction

Wherever you work, if you are interested in improving the quality of educational services, this book is designed to help you carry out a thorough evaluation of your institution, course or project and to assess your own performance. It has been written principally for those who work in adult and further education, whether in formal classes or informal learning groups; in colleges of further education or drop-in centres staffed by volunteers: wherever learning takes place. The main purpose of the book is to enable teachers to create and use a variety of mechanisms to evaluate their own work, assess the satisfaction of their students and find ways of improving the quality of the service they offer.

It will help you create a democratically run system of evaluation which will involve everyone – students, teachers and managers – in assessing the quality and value of learning experiences. Evaluation, as described in this book, empowers all who are involved in it, gives them a sense of ownership of the processes and, hence, a greater commitment to it.

If evaluation is to be effective, it must lead to change. The accumulation of data is only the first step in this process. It is not the purpose of this book to suggest how to effect change. But it is vital that this goal – implementing changes to continuously improve the quality of service – is never forgotten. Once data has been collected (using a wide range of techniques as described in the book) it must be carefully analysed by all those who have an interest in it – and this process should include the students. Then action plans for change (with timescales) must be created; the changes must be implemented and their effectiveness evaluated. In this way, evaluation plays its essential role in a curriculum planning cycle.

Many of the ideas in this book are drawn from my experiences during seven years of evaluating an educational project in Liverpool called *Second Chance to Learn*. This project offers courses to working class adults who care about what is happening on Merseyside and who want to understand the reasons for its decline and work out what part they can play in reversing it (see **M. Yarnit,** 1980 and **J. Edwards,** 1986). I was employed by the Workers' Educational Association to carry out a very detailed evaluation of *Second Chance to Learn,* and afterwards extended the evaluation approaches and techniques in a variety of educational settings on Merseyside and around the country.

Much of this work has been with relatively small-scale projects and courses in both the voluntary and statutory sectors. The approaches described in this guide and its appendices should be of immediate use to workers in similar settings. They could also be used for larger-scale institutional evaluation, with evaluation activities being carried out by course teams or other small groups of workers.

More recently, I have been involved in establishing a system of evaluation in a college of further education and in helping to implement a Local Education Authority system of Quality Assurance. These experiences have reaffirmed my belief that effective evaluation must begin in the classroom. It is necessary, however, to link teacher-led evaluation, as described in this book, to the requirements of LEAs and college managers, and so create complementary systems and activities. **Chapters 2** and **5** address this need.

Further guidance on institutional or city-wide evaluation can also be obtained from Elizabeth Whale (formerly co-ordinator of Birmingham's Quality Development Team) who has carried out evaluation for the city of Birmingham and is able to provide advice on organisation and the training of workers in evaluation method. Her address is on page 98.

Although this guide has been written for teachers and others working in the field of adult education, ideas in it can readily be adapted for use in youth and community work, within community groups, in schools,

in higher education: wherever people come together with some common purpose and where learning in its broadest sense takes place.
This guide is short and simple and is designed only to get you started. The large selection of appendices may provide you with ideas which can be used or modified.

New Developments in the Measurement of Quality

Although this book has been written mainly to assist teachers to carry out their own evaluation, this cannot be done in isolation. It is necessary to understand more about the context in which such evaluation takes place. In the late 1980's there has been a tremendous growth in the measurement of quality in adult and further education, led by the Department of Education and Science (DES) and the Department of Environment's Training Agency, amongst others. A bewildering range of 'quality systems' has been created with accompanying publications and, at times, a new vocabulary. In the remaining pages of this introduction I hope to explain these systems and help readers to understand the origins, purposes and limitations of them. This is not an easy task as the pace of development is rapid and the relationships between the systems are complex. Further reading from the reference list (see page 93) should prove helpful.

These new developments have much to offer anyone who wishes both to demonstrate the quality of existing services and to improve upon that quality. Equally, they have considerable limitations. I believe that in the coming years we must evolve an approach to evaluation which combines the democratic form of evaluation, as described in this book, with the requirements of government, LEAs and college managers for standardised quality measurement. To assist this process, I shall first briefly describe the new systems, then examine their shortcomings and finally demonstrate how the evaluation approaches outlined in this book can overcome some, at least, of these limitations and can be used in conjunction with the new systems.

The New Systems

In the last decade a new climate has been established. The public services must offer 'value for money' and 'freedom of choice' to potential 'customers'. Widespread changes have occurred in all the public services, health and transport, for example, as well as education. The Education Reform Act of 1988 has created self-managing colleges of further education, through its delegated budgeting arrangements. Governors responsible for colleges are under increasing local and national pressure to provide cost-effective, high quality services. Colleges must function as businesses, operating within defined budgets and competing with a growing number of private training agencies. In this new competitive climate, quality matters more than it has ever done. That quality must be demonstrated to potential customers (be they students or employers who purchase training for their workforces) and it must be continuously improved. New systems of 'quality assurance' and 'quality control' (both terms borrowed from industry) are being introduced to meet these requirements.

One of the first systems was introduced by the government. The Department of Education and Science produced a set of efficiency indicators (see **DES/WO**, 1987) known as Joint Efficiency Indicators, which are essentially *quantitative* measures of an institution's *efficiency*. They are cost-related and include, for example, target staff/student ratios, enrolment and completion rates and success rates in gaining qualifications or progressing to a job or higher education. By 1992 all colleges of further education will have to produce data which demonstrates their efficiency in relation to these indicators. These will be published by the DES in national 'league tables'. The measures will be used to assist in the allocation of resources by the DES and by LEAs responsible for the delegation of funds.

Efficiency alone is not enough to measure the value of education. The DES noted the need for measures of *effectiveness* and the Responsive College Programme has been developing a series of questionnaires to ascertain the level of 'client-satisfaction' (see **FESC**, 1988). The R.C.P. (funded by the Department of Employment's Training Agency and managed by the Further Education Unit) has produced a system known as SPOC/EPOC (Students'/Employers' Perceptions of Colleges). The questionnaires, which are administered at several points in the academic year, seek clients' opinions about the quality of service

4

offered. Several LEAs are using SPOC/EPOC systems throughout their institutions. Because all students (or employers) answer the same questions, comparisons can be made between courses and colleges.

It is argued, however, that a much broader approach to the measurement of quality is needed than that provided by the DES's efficiency indicators or by SPOC/EPOC. There has been a call for *Total Quality Management,* in response to which the FEU has produced an Educational Audit Reference Inventory (see **FEU**, 1989). This audit is extremely detailed and wide-ranging covering not only the clients' satisfaction with courses, but with the services of the whole institution (buildings, refreshments, support and guidance services etc.) and examining the effectiveness of the management structure.

Another response to this call has been the Training Agency's *Strategic Quality Management* system (see **J. Miller & S. Inniss**, 1990 and **J. Miller & A. Dower**, 1989). This system emphasises the notion of *service,* recommending that if teachers are to serve their customers (students), managers must shift from an "hierarchy based on status towards one based on service, where the 'subordinate' is seen as the manager's customer". In this system, definitions of quality (known as 'quality characteristics') are created, from which 'quality standards' are set and subsequently measured.

An institution which establishes one of these wide-ranging systems of evaluation can now choose to apply for the *British Standards Institute's BS5750* 'kitemark' of quality. Originally developed for use in industry, the BS5750 is being adapted for use in further education. An institution holding the BS5750 offers potential customers a guarantee of quality. Some of the newly-established Training and Enterprise Councils, which administer an ever-increasing proportion of the country's educational and training budgets, require that recipients of their funding possess the BS5750.

All of the systems described above have been devised for use in the further education sector and are not readily transferable to the adult and community education sectors. In the latter, the sheer size of the adult population who partake of these services, the extremely varied motivations and needs of the learners, and the vast range of courses offered, require much more flexible systems of evaluation. To meet this requirement, the Unit for the Development of Adult Continuing Education initiated a *Performance Indicators Project* (see **UDACE**, 1989). It is seeking, through a series of experimental projects, to develop a variety of new 'performance indicators' centred on "learner achievement, including social and personal development."

The interest in assessing quality of service, which is common to all the above developments, is a move to be welcomed, provided that appropriate indicators of quality are established and techniques for their measurement are developed. Complacency has, in the past, sometimes stunted the growth of new initiatives and some inadequate and inefficient services have continued unchallenged. At the same time, some of the most exciting developments have not been fully recognised, valued and replicated. Evaluation has its part to play in uncovering inadequacies and, equally, in demonstrating good practice.

Limitations of the New Systems
Whilst the new systems described above can undoubtedly assist in the improvement of both efficiency and effectiveness, they have serious limitations which must be both recognised and redressed.

One of the features common to these systems is that they are established and controlled by managers and can be described as 'top-down', reflecting the hierarchical structure of further and adult education. The DES, for example, has established the Joint Efficiency Indicators. LEAs decide what questions to ask their clients in the SPOC/EPOC systems. College managers decide what to 'audit' and measure in the Total Quality Management systems. Whilst it is appropriate for managers to set criteria and devise systems of measurement which meet their own needs for information to assist them in decision-making, this can only constitute a part of a complete evaluation.

When teachers, students (and employers) are not *actively* involved in setting criteria for measuring quality, there can be serious omissions, with a resulting imbalance. Students' needs and motivations are extremely varied and if these are not included in criteria, an inaccurate impression of quality will be gained.

6

Another consequence of a manager-led evaluation system is the lack of 'ownership' experienced by teachers and students. When students are asked to complete questionnaires whose purpose they do not understand, containing irrelevant questions, they do not comply wholeheartedly and the resulting data is often incomplete and inaccurate. Teachers asked to administer such questionnaires frequently see them as yet another burden heaped upon the shoulders of an already busy staff. There is widespread resentment of 'more paperwork'  m about its hidden purposes or whether it will anagers. It is remarkably easy to sabotage such ceit or omission. When students and teachers l in creating and managing evaluation systems, rely restricted. Inaccurate data is, moreover, seriously misleading to decision-makers.

Without a sense of ownership, there is little hope of real change taking place. When data is collected, for example in the SPOC/EPOC systems, turned into columns of figures by computer-operators and redistributed to staff some time later, it will often receive little more than a cursory glance and is almost never discussed with the students who supplied it. It needs to be properly analysed and discussed by *all concerned* if useful changes are to result from it.

The standardised questionnaires currently in use are, at best, blunt instruments; at worst, irrelevant. I have already noted the difficulty of establishing appropriate criteria across a wide range of courses and services offered to a varied student and employer population. There are additional difficulties. Large numbers of adults cannot read and write adequately to complete these questionnaires independently (either because they left school without acquiring sufficient skill or because they do not speak English fluently). Others who could complete them lack the motivation. Questionnaires are, moreover, difficult to construct (see **Chapter 3**). We must inevitably conclude that it would be most unwise to draw firm conclusions from questionnaire-based evaluation systems. Recognising these limitations should not automatically lead to the rejection of the various systems of evaluation. It should, instead, lead to a determination to use what is valuable in them and to improve areas of weakness. I hope to demonstrate how this can be done.

A Democratic System

The system of evaluation described in this book is a more demo-cratically controlled one. It could be described as 'bottom-up'. Teachers and students (and this could be extended to employers, too) are encouraged to establish their own criteria which arise out of their efforts to define their aims and objectives. They go on to develop their own, individually-tailored methods of measurement. These can include, but do not unduly rely upon, questionnaires. Students are encouraged to evaluate their courses and their teachers in a supportive, co-operative climate where all seek to improve the quality of the service. Thus a genuinely student-centred system of evaluation is created. Teachers, in turn, evaluate themselves and the effectiveness of their managers and the institutional systems which either assist or impede them in the delivery of good quality services.

A system like this empowers students and teachers. It motivates them by offering a feeling of ownership. Students and teachers feel they have some control over the processes; they can decide what to explore, how to do it and how to use what they find out. They understand its purpose and can enjoy creating evaluation systems which are relevant to their needs. When this happens, there is a much greater likelihood that productive changes will emerge and be wholeheartedly implemented.

The need for quantitative measures of efficiency must be recognised, so must the need for qualitative measures of effectiveness tailored to individual learning situations. Creating systems which bring these two elements together will not be easy. It will take many years of concentrated effort and adequate resourcing. Conflicts between hierarchical and democratic approaches will need to be recognised and resolved. This book offers an alternative and complementary approach to evaluation which encourages managers, teachers and students to find ways of working together. It recommends the establishing of Evaluation Steering Committees to control and direct evaluation systems. It describes a wide range of methods and offers suggestions for the staff development and training which will be necessary.

Whether you are a member of a small educational project or a manager of a large institution, you will find in the chapters which follow many practical ideas to help you begin evaluating the quality of your services. This will help to ensure that the new principle of *service* to customers becomes practice. The days when students had to fit into existing provision and make the best of it have gone. Learning programmes must now be tailored to the students' and employers' needs and evaluated upon the extent to which those needs have been met. Thus a genuinely student-centred style of learning and teaching can be implemented.

CHAPTER 1

Evaluation: What it is and why it matters

Definition

Evaluation can be defined in numerous ways. In one sense we evaluate all that we do all of the time whether we are working, gardening or watching the T.V. etc. We make judgements and adjust things accordingly. In this book I use the word to refer to a series of procedures carried out to collect information about learning experiences on the basis of which recommendations can be made to improve the quality of the services provided. It is organised, systematic and rigorous and involves the recording of information in some detail. At its best, it is designed with others, carried out with full participation and the results are widely disseminated, so that we can learn from good practice and from our mistakes. Evaluation shares knowledge and, therefore, power. For this reason it can cause anxiety.

There are several stages which will be explained in detail in the following chapters. These stages can be depicted as a continuous cycle.

See Evaluation Cycle diagram on page 12.

Evaluation Cycle

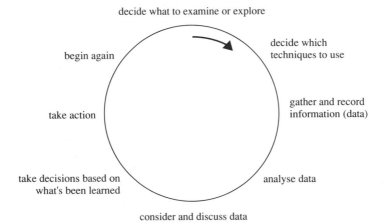

decide what to examine or explore

decide which
techniques to use

begin again

gather and record
information (data)

take action

take decisions based on
what's been learned

analyse data

consider and discuss data

Evaluation as described in this guide incorporates, but goes beyond, monitoring. When we monitor a service we employ a number of techniques to gather and record information. We may do this because we are required to do so by employers (e.g. keeping records of student attendance); or because we wish to check out the effectiveness of policies (e.g. proportions of men/women attending, if we are operating an equal opportunities policy). The information we gather from monitoring a service will contribute to the evaluation process. It frequently alerts us to problems which need further investigation. Evaluation involves assessing students' progress and achievements but goes much further than this by judging the value of that learning.

Evaluation is a tool – one of the most useful tools available for improving the quality of services. But, like any tool, it can be used effectively or not, depending upon the skill of the user. It can also be used for good or bad, depending upon the intentions of the user.

Evaluation – purposes

Evaluation has many purposes. When we evaluate a service we seek to describe and explain the experiences of students and teachers and then we make judgements about their value or effectiveness. We try to understand the *whole* experience of the learner or teacher, not just one part of it. We learn from this attempt; and our institutions can learn. If what is learned is then used by those with the authority to make decisions (and, of course, this is not always the case), the quality of the service is continuously improved. There can be many different reasons for evaluating a course or service, each offering different benefits. Some of these purposes are described below.

The processes can allow students, users or group members to become much more fully involved in decision-making because they come to understand the goals and intentions of teachers, providers or organisers. They have the opportunity to reflect and talk about their own goals and aspirations and they become actively involved in assessing whether these goals are being achieved. In this way, some of the barriers which exist between managers, teachers and students can be broken down and a more democratic, student or client-centred service is created. The traditionally hierarchical relationship between students and tutors and managers is altered. Evaluation as described in this book is a collective procedure with a genuine role for all.

Evaluation should always lead to more effective communication between all those involved in a project. It can involve, for example, the recording and exchange of information in the form of diaries, observations, reports, minutes or questionnaires. Communication with others outside the project can be greatly improved because it is a relatively short step to move from the recording of information to the writing of reports for other bodies. This has enormous implications. There are innumerable educational projects, community groups, youth clubs, etc. all over the country developing innovatory approaches. Yet how much of this experience is shared? The pace of development is slowed down tremendously and lessons have to be learned anew as the wheel is re-invented, time after time. As new staff replace old, the length of time spent upon induction of new workers could be greatly reduced, too, if the data gathered during evaluation was made available.

Chapter 1

Accountability, both to the public and to the users of particular services, is improved when projects are carefully evaluated and the information gathered is made available to others. Whilst information can be abused as often as it is well-used, the benefits overall outweigh the disadvantages. As we shall see later (in **Chapter 5**), safeguards can be built in to protect the interests of those who may feel threatened.

It is worth remembering that public services are increasingly being asked to justify their existence. Further and adult education is changing rapidly. Many local education authorities and voluntary bodies are facing cut-backs. The government and its agencies have set a climate where efficiency and cost-effectiveness must be demonstrated. Evaluation is becoming widespread. But usually this means that the funding bodies are carrying out the evaluation on their own terms and using their own criteria for success. Workers and users of the services often feel that these criteria are inadequate measures of success. If we wish to avoid being assessed solely by quantitative measures (for example, by the number of users who attend and the cost per student), it is vital that we take control of the evaluation processes ourselves. Workers and users should play a full part in determining the criteria for success. Qualitative criteria are just as important as quantitative ones.

It is vital that we take control of the evaluation processes ourselves.

14

Accountability is usually thought of as reporting to those in authority. Evaluation, as described in this guide, emphasises *the importance of being accountable to our students as well as our employers or funders.* If we fail our students in the delivery of our services, many of them will blame themselves, not us. They will attribute their failure to learn to their own weaknesses: *"I'm just stupid"* or *"I didn't work hard enough"*. They may give up with a sense of their own failure reaffirmed. Evaluation can help students to understand their own learning processes, judge the quality of their courses and develop the confidence to challenge and change situations.

Teachers often feel isolated in their work, in need of support, in need of the opportunity to think aloud, bounce ideas off others, test things out. Most good teachers actively try to improve their teaching by reading books, talking to colleagues or by attending courses if these are available. *Evaluation speeds up a teacher's learning processes.* A new idea can be tried out, carefully evaluated, refined, tried again. *'Action research'* is being carried out on a continuous basis with feedback from students. The sense of isolation diminishes. If the evaluation is conducted with colleagues, the level of support can be greater.

Evaluation can contribute to the development of learning theory (and, thereby, to improved teaching/learning). If we pick up a textbook on learning theory, it will often have been written by an academic, far removed from the practice of teaching and learning. There is no denying the value of much of this theory. But theory could be greatly enriched and of more immediate value to practitioners if those who teach and learn could contribute directly to its development. It might be more readable, too! In evaluating a course, learners are asked to reflect upon and discuss how best they learn, what barriers exist for them, etc. If this was carried out on a large scale and recorded, a wider audience could benefit from the insights gained. Even if it is not disseminated, those involved in the discussions would learn a great deal – theory would be developed.

Conclusion
It is vital that before evaluation is embarked upon, careful thought is

15

given to the purposes for which it is to be carried out. This may seem self-evident, but it does not always happen. There has been a tendency to be preoccupied with what should be evaluated and how it should be done without proper thought being given to the usefulness of the activity – the purpose of it. In America, where evaluation has been extensively practised for many years, a joint Committee of Standards for Educational Evaluation was established in 1972. It has met regularly since then and produced many useful guidelines. In 1980, Daniel Stufflebeam, a leading figure in the field of evaluation in America and a member of the Joint Committee of Standards for Educational Evaluation stated in an interview that four features should characterise evaluation. These are *utility, feasibility, propriety* and *accuracy* (in that order of importance). His statement can guide our thoughts as we plan to evaluate our work.

> '. . . *an evaluation should not be done at all if there is no prospect of it being useful to some audience. Second, it should not be done if it is not feasible to conduct in political terms, or practicality terms or cost-effectiveness terms. Third, they* (the Joint Committee of Standards for Educational Evaluation) *do not think it should be done if we cannot demonstrate that it will be conducted fairly or critically. Finally, if we can demonstrate that an evaluation will have utility, will be feasible and will be proper in its conduct, then they said we could turn to the difficult matters of the technical adequacy of the evaluation . . .'*
> **(D. Stufflebeam**, 1980)

It is important to note that getting the methodology right is the last of the four features. This does not imply that methodology is unimportant. Rather, it reverses an earlier trend in which methodological correctness has been elevated to such an extent that it controls and determines evaluation processes. *It is the purposes of evaluation which should determine methodology.* This fundamental principle can prove very disconcerting to bureaucratically inclined managers (or teachers) who believe that a universal measure of quality can and should be created so that comparable results can be produced. Like can be

16

usefully compared with like. But which two courses or sets of individuals are alike enough to make the comparisons valid in every respect?

If the principles of utility, feasibility and propriety are kept in the forefront of decision-making, the selection (or devising) of appropriate methodology becomes relatively straightforward. As we shall see in **Chapter 3,** the methodology does not lack rigour and, provided that a wide range of measures are used, valid results can be achieved.

Finally, whatever your reasons for embarking upon evaluation, you will discover that the ripples spread far wider than you originally envisaged.

CHAPTER 2

Evaluating yourself, your course and your institution

Introduction

Evaluation and appraisal are an essential part of adult education, strengthening the capacity of the student, the teacher and the institution to learn effectively. Every teaching/learning situation is different. It follows that every evaluation will be different too, as it must be tailored to meet the needs of individuals (both teachers and learners), of groups and, sometimes, of institutions. This chapter should help you to work out the most appropriate ways of establishing evaluation procedures for yourself, your course and your workplace. The principles of good practice which are set out in this chapter are transferable from individual self-appraisal (by a teacher or a manager) to group evaluation, whether this is carried out by a small group of teachers or by a whole institution (or even an education authority). The chapter focuses especially on how to go about taking decisions and recommends that some kind of decision-making committee (an *evaluation steering group*) should be set up at the outset.

Evaluation should, ideally, be carried out by a group of people who have a common interest in the development of a service. Setting up an evaluation team takes time, however: the wheels of change move slowly, especially in large, long-established institutions. You may work alone or in the kind of setting in which group evaluation would be impossible. The chapter begins, therefore, by exploring how an individual teacher can set about evaluating her/his work by means of self-appraisal and also by involving students in evaluating the success of the course and the teaching. This kind of group evaluation inside a class or course is an essential and relatively easy target for any teacher to achieve. Managers within institutions could employ similar approaches to evaluate their effectiveness, too. Evaluating yourself is always worthwhile: it could be the most significant step that can be taken to improve the quality of services. If teachers, or other staff, are reluctant to take this step, then any form of group or institutional appraisal is unlikely to succeed. Self-evaluation can, moreover, be incorporated into a broader evaluation if/when the opportunity arises.

Next, the chapter explores how a small group of people who work together to provide a service, can jointly establish evaluation procedures. Such a group may be employed on a particular educational project (such as *Second Chance to Learn* in Liverpool, whose experience of evaluation contributes much to this book). The small group could, alternatively, be part of a much larger institution, such as a group of lecturers in a polytechnic or college, each of whom spends some part of their time teaching a particular course or subject. However they are constituted, the group would need to establish decision-making mechanisms and find ways of co-ordinating and carrying out the evaluation activities. *Evaluation as a group activity* (below) offers suggestions to any small group of workers who decide they would like to evaluate themselves and their service.

Many teachers are employed by large institutions and may be unable or unwilling to evaluate their own particular areas of work in isolation. An evaluation of the whole institution may be called for. *Evaluating an institution* indicates some of the aspects of an institution which could be usefully evaluated and emphasises the need for effective control of the procedures through a widely-representative evaluation steering group.

Whether evaluation is carried out by an *individual*, or *small group*, or by an *institution*, it will be essential to create the right atmosphere. The chapter examines how this can be done and also offers practical guidance on how decisions about what to evaluate can be reached.

Evaluating yourself

Self-evaluation can begin with introspection and analysis. List your aims and objectives – what are you trying to achieve? What do you feel you *should* be spending your time on? Then, reflect upon how you actually spend your time. Write that down, too. Do the two match up? It is very unlikely that you will be able to answer 'yes'. So are you doing what you feel you should be, or does your time go on other activities? It is very hard to get an accurate impression of how you spend your time, rather like dieters estimating how much they eat: self-deception lurks.

It is very hard to get an accurate impression of how you spend your time.

So begin by keeping an accurate diary of a week, noting every activity you perform each day and how long you spend on it. This is time-consuming but very worthwhile. You may be in for some surprises. Decide how you want to change. *Set clear targets for yourself – write them down.* Try to repeat this exercise from time to time and monitor your progress.

To make the best use of this system of self-analysis, get together with a friend or work colleague if you can. Set aside an hour or two each month. Allocate the time equally between you, examining in turn what has happened to you in the intervening month (using a weekly log chart if you have kept one), exploring problems which have arisen and setting new targets for the month to come. This simple system can effect dramatic changes, the time used being amply repaid by better use of your remaining time.

You may like to use or adapt the simple self-appraisal questionnaires included in this guide (**Appendix 1a** and **1b** on pages 100 and 101). These are taken from **Paper 2304** of the **F.E.S.C.** publications, most of which are available free of charge. (See page 97 for publication details.)

Self-appraisal for a teacher must include reflection upon your effectiveness in preparing for and teaching classes or groups, even if you work in the most informal settings. You need to ask yourself a series of questions, and give yourself honest replies. **Appendix 2** (also from **F.E.S.C. Paper 2304**) lists a number of headings under which you should examine yourself. It has been prepared for teachers in colleges of education and so may require some adaptation for those who work in other settings.

Getting your students to help you evaluate yourself

Your effectiveness as a teacher can best be judged by your students' success in learning. By this I do not simply mean what skills they can perform, but the quality of the entire learning experience. Many of the techniques described in detail in **Chapter 3** can be used by any teacher who wishes to evaluate her/himself.

In order to judge how effective you are in your classroom, your students could be asked to complete, from time to time, a questionnaire similar to that presented in **Appendix 3** (page 103). This questionnaire was designed for the appraisal of lecturers by their students in colleges of further education. It is lengthy and may be inappropriate, but it can guide you in the construction of a more appropriate questionnaire. Note the precise questions and the rating scale for the answers (vague questions elicit vague replies). You might like to try rating yourself on your questionnaire before you analyse your students' responses, and then compare the outcomes.

Whatever methods you decide to use to involve your students in appraising you, the key to your success will lie in establishing the kind of relationship in which students feel safe enough to answer honestly.

... the kind of relationship in which students feel safe enough to answer honestly.

This requires great skill on the part of the teacher, who must not only try to ensure anonymity (difficult with handwritten answers) but must also persuade the students that honest answers are welcome. Thus, critical comments should not be seen as criticism of the teacher, but as helpful guides to improvement. It takes time for most student groups to get used to this way of working and relating to a teacher. The first occasions when students appraise their teachers are unlikely to be very honest, but this usually changes with practice.

If you begin immediately to use any of the ideas in this chapter, the quality of your service and, subsequently, your job-satisfaction will be improved. You may be powerless or reluctant to go further than this in the evaluation of your work. But if you are part of a group who work together on a course or project you will need to consider a number of issues before proceeding any further. The remainder of this chapter deals with these issues.

Evaluation as a group activity: shared decision-making

To get started, someone usually has to take the initiative and get it organised. Perhaps that's you. This does not mean you will immediately start devising questionnaires, interviewing others, etc. Because *evaluation must be part of your working processes,* it is vital that many people are involved and that decision-making (about what is to be looked at, who will do the work involved, and so on) is shared.

It is important to set up a *steering group* or an *evaluation committee* to take the decisions, rather than leave it all in the hands of one or two people. The group should have representatives of paid workers, users, volunteers and, maybe, managers. Try not to exclude any interest-groups, because *the evaluation will be most successful if everyone feels involved and can contribute to decision-making.* Co-operation in all the following stages will then be much greater.

The function of the steering group will be to take decisions about what is to be evaluated, when, by whom, with what resources, in what ways etc. The group should draw up a timetable of activities (estimating the time each stage will take) and should regularly monitor progress, setting new targets as and when appropriate. **Chapter 5** explores in detail the role of the steering group and the important issues which it will need to discuss and resolve.

Some educational projects already have an appropriate decision-making structure. The Workers' Educational Association, for example, is democratically organised with Branches throughout the country in which students take decisions, with a class secretary or representative reporting to the Branch and field staff. Such a structure lends itself very easily to the co-ordination of evaluation processes. In an institution with a more hierarchical structure (such as most colleges of further education) the act of setting up the committee could itself prove problematic as it may pose a challenge to existing structures of management and control.

Step one in the diagram on page 12 says 'decide what to examine or explore'. Whether you are working alone, with a small group or as part of a large-scale institutional evaluation, the same procedures can help you decide. The following questions may help you structure your programme:

What do we want to know?
Why? What use will we make of it?
How can we find out?
Who will be involved?
When will we do it?
What resources will be needed?
How will we communicate what we learn, and to whom?

When you talk with others about what to evaluate, you may well feel overwhelmed by the scale of it all. The broader the composition of the evaluation steering group, the wider and more comprehensive the range of questions will be. In the early stages, it is best to 'brainstorm', to encourage all ideas. Then it is very important to carefully prioritize. What do you *need* to know urgently? Why?

Appendix 4 provides a set of checklists which are often used in training workshops with staff who are about to embark upon an evaluation of their services. They could be used by the steering group in the early stages of 'brainstorming' and prioritizing.

Some common themes which are often pursued are:

Goals
What are the goals of the project, course, service or organisation?
Who decides these goals?
Is there a consensus, or are the goals of teachers/organisers different from those of others involved?
Are the goals achieved?

Students/Services
Who comes to use the service?
What is their motivation?
Are they the 'target' group which the service was set up to provide for?
What do the users gain from the service and how does it affect their lives?

25

What problems do they encounter and why do some leave without making full use of the service?
How can the service be improved?

Operation
How does the service operate?
What is its management structure?
How are decisions made and by whom?
How effectively does it operate?
How could it be improved?

After you have decided what to evaluate, consider the methods described in **Chapter 3** and opt for those you feel most comfortable with and which seem to you to be most appropriate for the job in hand. The availability of time and resources will be an important factor in your deliberations. Avoid the temptation to do too much at once or you may lose heart. Start small, succeed, then extend your evaluation programme. Seek to be creative so that the process is stimulating and enjoyable for all concerned.

Evaluating an institution

It can be very beneficial to evaluate the institution in which courses are provided: the management, administration, ancillary services and the general environment. It becomes increasingly necessary to do so, as the FEU publication **Towards an Educational Audit** (**FEU**, 1989) clearly indicates. Evaluating an institution is an extremely complex undertaking with numerous pitfalls awaiting the unwary enthusiast. **C. Adelman** & **R. J. Alexander** (1982) offer invaluable insights into the experience. Their book should be read by anyone considering institutional evaluation.

No major evaluation of this sort should ever be started until an evaluation steering group of some sort has been established. Great care must be taken to ensure that all interests are properly represented. Unless everyone involved feels they have the opportunity to air their opinions and concerns and contribute to decisions, the evaluation is most unlikely to be worthwhile.

Much of the evaluation of an institution will centre around the work of teachers and the educational service they deliver. It can best be carried out by small groups of staff (as described in *Co-ordinating and carrying out evaluation,* below). It is possible for each small group to establish its own steering group to facilitate decision-making and oversee the day-to-day processes. Appropriate evaluation techniques (as described in **Chapter 3**) could be selected and implemented.

But when an institution is to be evaluated, the process goes far beyond the examination of individual courses or programmes within it. All educational institutions have existing data collection systems (often referred to as Management Information Systems). Many institutions are now adopting ready-designed quality assurance systems including sets of questionnaires seeking students and sometimes employers' perceptions of courses (these are explained in the **Introduction** and are known as SPOC and EPOC). An evaluation steering group must take into account these existing systems and decide how to incorporate them into its own work to avoid duplication. It also has to examine the limitations of these systems and so avoid being restricted by them. It must decide what else should be explored in a full-scale evaluation. As well as examining course content and delivery, much else can be considered. The following paragraphs deal with some of the possibilities.

Meetings of teaching staff and of the various college management committees can be observed from time to time in order to understand how decisions are made and what influences them. The teaching staff must have the chance to evaluate and comment upon factors which influence their work – in particular the performance of their manager, head of department or management committee. This is an important part of the overall picture which is being built up. It can prevent teachers from feeling that all the problems are their own fault or responsibility, or that a report may apparently indicate this without allowing them to 'set the record straight.' If teaching staff have much to learn from students, then, equally, managers have much to learn from staff. Students, teachers and the managers themselves should all participate in this evaluation.

Students can be asked to evaluate the ancillary services provided by the caretaking/cleaning staff and the administrative staff. Student guidance and counselling services, the library services, creche facilities, refectory services are all part of the infrastructure of an institution which directly affects the overall quality of service which is offered. Suitability of location, timing of classes, costs, publicity, access for people who often suffer from discrimination (such as women, members of ethnic minority groups, the disabled) are all legitimate areas for exploration when an evaluation of services is being undertaken.

Teaching staff, managers and administrators can all participate in evaluating the management and administration systems of the institution. Senior staff can appraise themselves and their peers, and the teaching staff can be invited to evaluate the performance of those who direct and control their work. Senior staff need to set an example of willingness to be evaluated and readiness to change. If they do not, they can hardly expect others to participate enthusiastically in evaluation procedures.

The morale of staff can often be raised by enabling them to participate more fully in decision-making. Teaching, administrative, cleaning and other servicing staff can provide valuable recommendations to improve the efficiency of an institution and the quality of the services it provides. The practice of asking staff to make recommendations and involving them in decision-making has been successfully operated in many enlightened industries. It is time for the public services to catch up.

This brief answer to the question of what an evaluation of an institution can encompass serves to indicate the broad range of possibilities. Each option would require time, resources and training for the staff involved. The role of the steering group would be to ensure that the best choices are made.

Co-ordinating and carrying out evaluation

Evaluation works best when the practitioners of the service are fully involved in carrying out the evaluation procedures. Ideally, therefore, the classroom teachers should play a key role in evaluating their courses. In this way they are brought into dialogue (whether verbally or through written answers) with their students. They receive immediate feedback upon the quality of the service from its consumers. Evaluation thus becomes part of the planning and teaching cycle in which teachers are involved. They are much more likely to take note of and act upon what students have to say when they themselves play a part in deciding what should be explored and what questions should be asked, and when they read and hear the answers.

Nevertheless, when a group of teachers work as a team, (and when the team is part of a larger institution such as a college or a district of the W.E.A.), steps must be taken to organise and co-ordinate the evaluation and to train participating teachers and managers. It is often sensible to allocate the responsibility for co-ordinating the evaluation to an individual or a small group of people. Care must be taken, though, to ensure that evaluation activities do not become marginalised and ignored by the majority.

If one person is to be given the responsibility for co-ordinating evaluation activities, who should this person be? There may be a number of options:

(a) Someone already in charge – a head of department or senior worker, perhaps. This could cause great problems because it is unrealistic to expect workers to be open and honest in talking about their shortcomings, or to expect students to be critical, if they know that someone's job prospects can depend on what is said or written.

(b) A worker who has no authority over others. This could be a much better choice, especially if the person is respected. It must be recognised, however, that once a person starts to evaluate a project and becomes to some extent the holder of knowledge, there is a tendency for her/him to assume power, which must be consciously and actively resisted.

(c) Students/users could carry out the evaluation themselves rather than participate in exercises devised by someone else. Some form of training would almost certainly be needed. Can you reasonably expect someone to take on these responsibilities without payment? Students could come to feel exploited by the scale of what is required. These difficulties would need a full discussion.

29

(d) An outsider, unconnected with the service, could be appointed and paid for with a special grant. A post-graduate university student with an interest in your area of work might be suitable. Whilst there are definite advantages in bringing someone in from the outside who has no vested interest, there are also very real disadvantages. The person may have little understanding of, or empathy with, the project; will have to spend some time familiarising her/himself; may have conflicting interests, and will almost certainly prove more costly. The staff are more likely to disassociate themselves from the evaluation processes and so the potential for change may be greatly reduced.

(e) Most often the evaluation is initiated and carried out by one or more workers who are keen to improve the service. If this is what happens, steps must be taken to ensure that they do not work in isolation. Working to an evaluation committee or steering group as described above can overcome most difficulties.

No matter who takes on the responsibility for organising an evaluation and making it happen, all those who work/teach will have an active part to play if methods such as those described in **Chapter 3** are adopted. No special qualifications are needed to evaluate a scheme. Evaluators certainly do not need to be experienced researchers. Personal qualities such as the ability to listen, to empathise, to ask questions and relay information in an unthreatening manner – combined with good organisation and the ability to record information clearly – are much more important.

Effective evaluators need to be flexible and open, willing to adapt and change their approach and methodology to meet the varying needs of different institutional systems, different managers, teachers and students. They should be capable of approaching every evaluation situation with an open mind, ready to abandon pre-conceived ideas based upon previous experiences. They need to be effective trainers too, because every evaluation presents opportunities to train workers and managers. Above all, a positive attitude towards the services being evaluated is needed.

To sum up, it could be a good idea to allocate time to one or more workers in a project (provided they have no position of authority over the others) to co-ordinate the evaluation processes. A group of students/users could take part in the planning and carrying out of the processes. Some professional advice and assistance (if needed) could be obtained from an 'evaluation consultant' – a person with experience of research and/or evaluation – who can offer technical assistance in, for example, the drafting and analysis of questionnaires. All of these could be guided and directed by the steering group, which properly represents the interests of all those who have reason to be involved. Everyone must feel they 'own' the evaluation, that it is to be for their benefit. Conversely, no one should feel that it is being done to them against their will. If they do, they will learn nothing from it and may even seek to sabotage it.

Creating the right atmosphere

Whether an evaluation is to be conducted by an individual, a small group or an institution, it will only succeed when there is a feeling of 'ownership' and trust. It is not easy to create the right atmosphere. Evaluation can cause anxiety to some people. Information is about to come to light (or be confirmed) which could be unpleasant or even put jobs at risk. It is difficult, but vitally important, to reduce the element of threat. To do this, there should be an opportunity for all to voice concerns and fears and for safeguards to be built in before the work begins. The steering group (or evaluation committee) must seek to resolve some of the questions raised in **Chapters 4** and **5** of this book.

Whoever carries out the various activities must treat everyone with respect, but must not sacrifice honesty or rigour in an attempt to save someone's feelings. This balance can be difficult to achieve. No one should be exempted from the processes, especially those who may be given responsibility for organising the evaluation.

It may well be necessary to 'sell' evaluation as a concept to colleagues or managers. Some of the arguments which could be employed have already been discussed **(Chapter 1)**. The most successful way of convincing others, especially in a large institution such as a college, is to carry out a small-scale evaluation, demonstrating its usefulness. A 'pilot' of this kind would also allow you to uncover any particular difficulties and work on solutions, before carrying out a full-scale exercise.

No one should be exempted from the processes.

Evaluation should be approached thoroughly. However small-scale, attention must be paid to detail. Everyone involved must feel they are being taken seriously. A casual, sloppy approach would not succeed. There is a great deal of difference between informality of approach (which is often preferable) and carelessness.

When recommendations for change emerge they must be implemented wherever possible, and full explanations offered if they cannot be carried out. They must never be ignored, otherwise participants in the evaluation (be they staff or students) will feel that the exercise was a waste of time and will not co-operate in future.

Finally, in order to create the right climate, attention must be paid to group processes. Relationships within a steering group, amongst colleagues, between students and staff, amongst students (always of central importance) will be of increasing importance during an evaluation. Many groups would benefit from learning more about how to work effectively together. When groups of students carry out review exercises, they may need to be trained in group processes, so that all can express their viewpoints, time is allocated fairly, and opinions are accurately noted down and/or reported back. Part of the evaluation itself should involve the exploration of group processes and their effects upon the quality of the service. This guide does not attempt to offer ideas on how to work effectively in groups. There are many excellent publications available which could be studied by participants.

Conclusion

It is apparent that evaluation is a complex activity and one which requires careful thought and planning. This should not deter anyone from undertaking it. Neither should it be allowed to unduly delay the start of evaluation activities. Although many issues must be carefully considered, endless hours spent 'in committee' will kill off all enthusiasm. In most educational experiences you learn most by doing. Evaluation is no exception. Provided that the right kind of decision-making mechanisms are put in place, most of the issues can be dealt with as they arise, and the satisfaction derived from carrying out evaluation activities will motivate everyone concerned.

CHAPTER 3

Course evaluation methods

"There is no one best way to conduct an evaluation . . . every evaluation situation is unique. Evaluation needs to be situationally responsive rather than methodologically rigid and orthodox."
M. Q. Patton (1981)

Introduction

There are a great many techniques which can be used when carrying out an evaluation. This chapter lists and describes a wide range of techniques or methods (and the advantages and disadvantages of each). The techniques described here can all be used in order to evaluate the effectiveness of courses, but they can easily be adapted for use in evaluating any other aspect of an institution, such as the effectiveness of its marketing, its educational guidance service or its administrative back-up.

It is important to select those techniques which would seem best to fit in with the ethos of the class, group, project or institution, and best fulfil the purposes of the evaluation. A technique which would be appropriate for evaluating a university class of 150 attending formal lectures would be unlikely to suit a small group of students attending adult basic education classes. A technique for finding out why students leave courses would be different from one designed to ascertain the effectiveness of a new range of materials or a new way of delivering a course.

The techniques in this chapter all rely upon words as the means of describing experiences. In some groups, visual approaches such as drawing and video could provide an alternative way of conducting evaluation. There is no doubt that some techniques are much more formal than others. Just as the experienced and thoughtful teacher will select the best teaching/learning approaches for each group or individual, evaluation techniques need to be equally carefully chosen.

In order to carry out evaluation, you do not need to undergo lengthy training in research methods. It is not necessary to be able to measure statistical significance or use computers to analyse data. Most of the methods described in this chapter are extensions of everyday common-sense procedures.

No one method is sufficient in itself. The use of a variety of methods will lead to a fuller and more accurate understanding of a course. **Parlett & Hamilton** (1972 and 1977) describe evaluation as the 'illumination' of a learning situation. You wish to shed light on a course/project in order to understand it better. The more 'torches' you are able to shine upon it, the better you will be able to see into every nook and cranny. The more people who hold those torches and the wider the variety of angles from which the torches are shone, the fuller the description will be.

In an evaluation, use as wide a range of the methods described in this chapter as you can. Your choice will be affected by financial resources (some methods require a typist/paper/postage whilst others require just a little time);who you will be working with; the service you are evaluating; time available. *Begin with a few simple activities and build up your confidence as you go.* Soon you will find yourself wanting to adapt the ideas recommended in this book and devise your own.

It is important to get as many people as possible to 'hold the torches', too. In other words, ask colleagues, students, managers to think about what should be examined; involve them in carrying out some of the procedures. Students in adult education classes, for example, can become the 'researchers'. They can learn how to write questionnaires, carry out interviews, analyse the data, write up their findings and present them to others. The activity can be an extremely valuable and enjoyable one for all concerned. It can often produce a more accurate and truthful set of findings because students have undergone the experiences which they are now evaluating, so they have different insights to those of the class teachers or organisers of the service.

Evaluation needs to be carried out on a regular basis because however scrupulously it is conducted, a wholly accurate picture can never be drawn. And even if it could be, things would change. *Evaluation must be a continuous process.*

One of the greatest problems posed by evaluation is that of *defining and measuring 'success'*. Success in educational terms has almost always been equated with passing tests or public examinations, or going on to other forms of education afterwards. Students are also increasingly being assessed upon their competence in performing skills (manual or mental activities). Does this mean that students on courses where there is no form of assessment cannot be successful? What if a student comes to a course for a variety of reasons (not simply to gain a qualification) as so many adult learners do? If students participate in an educational activity in order to become more confident generally, to make friends, to meet people, to help with their children's education, to explore and develop their creativity, then tests of information acquired and memorised will be both irrelevant and inappropriate. New definitions of success, and new methods of measuring it must be devised. Evaluators must rise to this very difficult challenge. In 1989 NIACE published a document produced by the Unit for the Development of Adult Continuing Education (UDACE) which acknowledges this challenge and seeks to address it. UDACE launched a development project which 'seeks to examine the extent to which learners' achievements can be described, assessed and credited . . . (and) could lead to the development of a set of performance indicators centred on learner achievement'. (**UDACE**, 1989, page 18).

The starting point for definition and subsequent measurement of success must include the students' goals. In this chapter, under the heading of *At the Start,* a number of methods for finding out students' goals are explained. During the course a wide range of techniques can be used to measure the extent to which these goals are being met. These provide a measure of the quality of the course. Meeting students' goals is just a part of assessing the quality of the service, but a very important one. Other techniques to assess quality are also explained in the chapter, eg. observation of teachers' performances. Further measures, such as pass rates in examinations, access to jobs and/or higher education may also help to build up an accurate picture of quality. It is always valuable to follow up students some time after a course ends to see what has happened to them, what impact the course has had upon them, and to seek their views of the course with the benefit of hindsight.

By using a wide range of evaluation techniques as described in this chapter, an accurate assessment of the quality of the service can be obtained, without resorting to pre-course and post-course testing or other similar traditional methods of assessing the effectiveness of a learning experience.

Choosing the best methods

The table on page 39 lists some of the more frequently used methods of evaluation. They are organised under four headings:

1 *At the Start.* These procedures enable you to establish the goals of all those involved in offering and using the service. They provide you with a base-line which will be referred to in all subsequent stages as you evaluate the success of courses in fulfilling these goals.

2 *During the Course.* This offers a wide range of methods which should be used at regular intervals throughout a course. The results of these enquiries should be used in order to improve the course as it goes along *(Formative Evaluation).*

3 *At the End.* These evaluation methods should be used as the course nears its end, enabling you to produce a 'course report' *(Summative Evaluation)* and to shape future courses.

4 *Post-Course Evaluation.* These techniques can be used months or years after a course has ended. They are essential, often offering the most accurate evaluation of the value of a course.

The methods are numbered (1 to 20) in the table – but many methods are repeated during the four stages of evaluation. In the pages which follow, each method is described once. As well as a description of the methods, some of the advantages and disadvantages of each are explored, enabling you to make the most appropriate choices. This is not an exhaustive list. Skilful evaluators soon learn to adapt methods or create new ones.

METHODS OF EVALUATION

AT THE START
1	**Defining Students' goals by**
1a	**Group Discussion**
1b	**Questionnaires**
1c	**Individual Interviews**
2	**Defining goals of teachers and managers** (by same methods)

DURING THE COURSE
3	**Group Review Sessions**
4	**Questionnaires**
5	**Individual Interviews**
6	**Case Studies**
7	**Observation of Classes**
8	**Keeping Diaries and Log Books**
9	**Regular Evaluation Sheets**
10	**Course Records** (registers, students' work, minutes of meetings)
11	**Informal Approaches**

AT THE END
12	**Testing Students**
13	**Displays of Work**
14	**Group Reviews**
15	**Individual Interviews**
16	**Questionnaires**

POST-COURSE EVALUATION
Follow up studies of student destinations and course results by
17	**Questionnaires**
18	**Individual Interviews**
19	**Recall Meetings**
20	**Informal Approaches** (unplanned meetings and conversations)

Chapter 3

AT THE START

Finding out people's goals is a vital first step, because only when you know what they hope to achieve, can you define and begin to measure 'success'. You need to be clear about your own goals, those of your students, those of your colleagues and those of your funders. Your approach can be very informal or highly structured, as best fits the group or individual. You can find out goals by asking people individually or by asking them to discuss their goals within the group. You could also ask them to record their answers on paper or use a cassette. There are pros and cons with all these different approaches, as we will see in the following pages.

1a & 1b Defining Students' Goals by Group Discussion and Questionnaires

You can ask students to write or think about their answers to these or similar questions, *"Why did you decide to apply for a place on this course?"* and *"What do you hope to achieve?"* A group discussion can follow. Take notes of their points. Later, using these notes (and their written answers) you could construct a simple questionnaire which lists each of the statements of what they hope to achieve. Beside each there could be a series of boxes, (very important to me/reasonably important to me/not important to me). Students can be asked to consider each statement and tick the box which most closely resembles their feelings.

Analysis of the data is quick and easy, yielding percentages which indicate just how important various items are to individual students and to the group as a whole. It is easy to see both similarities and differences between group members. When tutors have also presented their goals (see page 42 later), comparison of students' and tutors' goals may prove very illuminating. Although many goals may be shared, their relative importance can differ greatly. Students and tutors can be given access to each others' conclusions and, as a result, can discuss and negotiate with clarity. A process of this kind is essential to those courses or services where no pre-set syllabus or activities are followed. Negotiation of the syllabus cannot be successful unless the various parties involved have had the opportunity to think clearly about what they hope to achieve and can present their ideas coherently to one another.

Advantages

i) All students become clearer about what they wish to achieve and this clarity can motivate them towards success.

ii) Tutors understand better the needs of the group as a whole and of individuals.

iii) Negotiation of curriculum is facilitated.

iv) Group discussion at an early stage gives students insights into each others' hopes and needs. It can broaden horizons immediately and frequently assists in the development of good relationships within a group.

v) Students feel that their views matter, right from the start. Barriers are thereby broken down between students/tutors.

Disadvantages

i) Most students find it quite difficult to express goals clearly when they first attend a class. In many cases, what they say soon changes and the procedure must be repeated regularly as horizons extend.

ii) Some students find this approach intimidating. They expect teachers to make all decisions and see consultation as a weakness/lack of professionalism on the part of the tutor.

iii) Questioning students about their needs and expectations creates an assumption that they will be fully met. It may not be possible to fulfil these expectations.

iv) This process could prove more difficult to engage in on a 'roll-on, roll-off' course with a changing student population.

1c Defining Students' Goals by Individual Interviews

These are valuable if conducted either before a course begins (if an interview is held) or very early on. Tutors usually interview each individual student but, alternatively, students could interview each other in pairs and record information.

Advantages

i) Students and tutors can quickly clarify individual goals and needs. Work can begin immediately to ensure that students experience some success.

ii) Students recognise and respond to being treated as individuals. This encourages and motivates them, especially those who are very nervous.

41

iii) If the course does not fulfil a student's needs and aspirations, the curriculum may be able to be altered, or the student can be advised about other, more suitable, courses.

iv) The written record can be used at regular intervals to assess progress. As targets are met, new ones can be selected.

Disadvantages

i) This is very time-consuming. Though it is time well spent as it establishes excellent relationships, many tutors simply could not embark on it.

ii) Some students find it hard to articulate their needs and goals and may say what they think is expected of them.

It would be possible to combine both individual interviews and group discussion when you attempt to find out your students' goals.

2 Defining Goals of Teachers and Managers

The same procedures can be used with teachers as are used with students. A group of teachers who all work together providing the same course (or set of courses) can be asked to share ideas about their goals, and later endorse these in a questionnaire. Teachers can also be encouraged to prioritize their various goals. It is most unlikely that a consensus will ever be reached but the process leads to much greater mutual understanding and individual clarity.

Managers can follow similar procedures, too. When all three groups (students, teachers and managers) have clarified and stated their goals, it is most illuminating for all concerned to arrange for their statements to be exchanged and discussed. This should only be done, however, with the consent of all concerned, otherwise the basic rule of confidentiality will have been broken.

Advantages

i) Teachers (or managers) become clearer about their own goals.

ii) They also understand the goals of their colleagues and how these relate to their own goals.

iii) This enhanced level of communication and mutual understanding should lead to more unity of purpose and assist teachers in their planning of course content and activities.

iv) When the teachers' (or managers') goals are communicated to students and when students (through the processes described in 1a, b and c above) are clearer about their own goals, real negotiation over course content and method can take place.

v) When the teachers' goals are clearly communicated to students, the students are in a much better position to evaluate the effectiveness of the course and the teaching.

Disadvantages

i) There may not be consensus or unity of purpose. Disagreements and tensions between staff who do not share common goals may be exacerbated.

ii) The process relies heavily upon teachers' ability to express themselves verbally and/or in writing.

iii) It can be difficult to find the time to get together all teachers concerned to discuss goals. And the process needs repeating from time to time as goals can change.

DURING THE COURSE

3 Group Review Sessions

The 'group review' is one of the simplest and most effective ways of obtaining a wealth of information and recommendations for improving a course. The method is quite straightforward. Students discuss together their answers to questions supplied by tutors. (See **Appendix 5** for a sample of questions used in *Second Chance* reviews, with accompanying instructions to students, and **Appendix 6,** a list of useful questions which can be asked.) Large groups of students should be divided into smaller groups (of 5 or 6) and asked to choose a chairperson (who ensures everyone gets a fair chance to contribute and also that all questions get answered in the allotted time) and a reporter who will later feed back the replies to the full group. At this stage it is best if tutors are not present, thereby allowing a more honest and open discussion. It may be necessary to provide training for the students in group processes and the roles of chair and reporter, in order to ensure that these groups function well. Small groups then come back together and, with their tutors, discuss their conclusions and recommendations.

The tutors' role is to listen and answer questions if asked. If time permits, a middle stage could be inserted where all student groups get together first to discuss what they wish to tell tutors.

Advantages
i) All individual students' comments are reported back anonymously by the group reporters – usually ensuring greater frankness.
ii) Discussion with other students helps individuals to understand their own and others' learning processes. It also helps to extend students' goals and horizons and allows support and encouragement to be offered.
iii) Students develop confidence in evaluating their tutors (and criticising is part of such an evaluation) and they have the opportunity to articulate ideas, challenge and negotiate with tutors – thus reducing the 'hierarchy' of many educational establishments and other services.

Disadvantages
i) Some quieter individuals cannot participate in group discussions and therefore inaccurate overall impressions may be gained.

Some quieter individuals cannot participate in group discussions.

ii) Poor chairing or reporting back will seriously impede the success of this method. Even after training in group skills, the problem may still exist.
iii) Views may be misunderstood and misrepresented. The individual then must either remain silent or lose her/his anonymity in correcting the statements.
iv) Students often find it embarrassing and difficult to offer criticism face to face with a tutor and so the spokesperson may not make a full, truthful report of the group's comments.

4 Questionnaires

Writing a questionnaire (or an 'opinionaire' as they are sometimes called) is not as difficult as many people fear. If you decide to use questionnaires as part of an evaluation (and they are very worthwhile), you do not have to do it alone. Talk to colleagues and students and ask them, *"What questions would you ask?"* Look at questionnaires in popular magazines etc. and compare different layouts.

It is a good idea to include both *closed* and *open* questions. Closed questions require 'yes'/'no' (and perhaps 'don't know') boxes. These are quick and easy to analyse (important if you have a lot of people to collect answers from) and relatively easy for students to answer – requiring no written expression. They are, however, sometimes frustrating to students who may not fully understand them and who feel the boxes do not offer proper scope for their response. Closed questions are, therefore, more suitable for gathering factual information rather than opinion seeking. Open questions can be used to ask students for their opinion or for recommendations and require answers in sentences or note form. A combination of open and closed questions works well e.g:

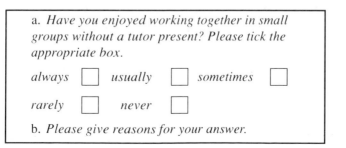

a. *Have you enjoyed working together in small groups without a tutor present? Please tick the appropriate box.*

always ☐ *usually* ☐ *sometimes* ☐

rarely ☐ *never* ☐

b. *Please give reasons for your answer.*

Then leave a space of a few lines for the answer. The size of the space you leave will indicate the length and detail of reply you would like. (A more detailed explanation of how to write a questionnaire appears in **Appendix 7** and a sample of a questionnaire used on *Second Chance* in **Appendix 8.**)

A word of caution about the length of a questionnaire is necessary. It is all too easy to produce a 6, 8 or 10 page questionnaire which would take a couple of hours and a good deal of writing skill to answer. Questionnaires seem to grow and grow. If, as a result, only a tiny proportion fill them in, the results will be of little value. Restrict your questions, however hard this may be and, perhaps, follow up particularly intriguing themes in individual or group interviews. Take care, too, in designing the questionnaire. You may discover later that you have omitted essential questions, or produced a set of data which is very complicated to analyse. Running a small 'pilot' first can ensure this does not happen.

Advantages
i) Everyone has the chance to say what they wish without being influenced by others. Every voice can be heard, giving a more accurate picture overall.
ii) Students will have time to ponder privately before they reply – especially if questionnaires can be taken away and returned later.
iii) Anonymity can be preserved, if desired (though handwriting could be a 'give-away').
iv) If additional questions about age, gender etc. are added, accurate analysis can be made to ascertain the relevance of such factors.
v) If large numbers of students are involved, questionnaires will probably be the only feasible way to collect information. This is especially true if you wish to contact students after they have left a course.

Disadvantages
i) Reading and writing skills are essential. It can, moreover, be very hard for anyone to express complex ideas in a few sentences and the attempt is often abandoned! Some students find questionnaires imposing, even threatening.

46

ii) It is hard to write complex questions in a simple, unambiguous way to avoid posing 'leading questions' which indicate to the students the answers you would like to hear.

iii) Students can only answer the questions you have asked! Other, perhaps more valuable, insights may be missed. Sometimes the analysed data tells you little you did not already know.

iv) Analysis can prove very difficult, especially if you use lots of *open* questions.

vi) There is often a poor response rate, especially if they are taken home or sent out by post, and so the results are unrepresentative. Questionnaires are often left to the end of a course and taken away by students. The response rate is then usually very poor.

vii) Paper and perhaps postage can prove expensive.

5 Individual Interviews

To fully understand a complex situation nothing can replace individual in-depth interviews. Open-ended questions can be asked and any aspect of the answers can be followed up by further questions. Individual interviews afford the opportunity to further explore ideas and queries which might have been raised in group reviews or questionnaires.

With a very small student group you may be able to interview all course members. If not, it is important to interview as representative a sample of students as possible. For example, if one third of the group are men, then one third of the interviewees should be men. If age seems relevant, then try to ensure a proportion of interviewees come from the different age groups represented on the course.

Even though individual interviews can follow a variety of paths, it is very important to think out and write down questions in advance (see **Appendix 9**), otherwise the conversation may soon stray to irrelevant areas and afterwards you will realise you forgot to ask about all kinds of important points. Either jot notes of the replies given or, preferably, record the interview on a cassette. This allows you to converse more naturally and ensure you don't omit relevant points, as you may when taking notes. If you do use a cassette, make sure you can operate it correctly and your interviewee feels happy about it.

You should offer all interviewees the chance to read your transcript of the tape or your write-up of the interview and you should permit anonymity if desired. (**Appendix 10** offers guidance on how to prepare for and carry out an interview. It also offers simple tips on the use of cassette recorders.) Interviewing is a skill which must be learned. Group training sessions on interview technique can be very productive. You can use some of the questions you intend to ask in a role-play exercise. If video is available, role-play of interviews can be played back to the group and techniques analysed and improved upon.

Advantages
i) In the hands of a skilful interviewer, there is no better way of achieving a full understanding of a student's opinions and experiences.
ii) You have an opportunity to follow up any comment which seems relevant or any answer you do not fully understand. This results in a much deeper level of understanding of the interplay of various factors upon each individual's experience of learning.

Disadvantages
i) It is very time-consuming. Each interview may take an hour or more and transcribing one hour of tape can take 3 to 6 hours.
ii) The success of the interview depends heavily upon interviewing skills and to some extent upon the articulacy of the interviewee.
iii) If the sample is badly constructed it may not prove very representative of the student group as a whole.
iv) The interviewee may find it hard to give critical answers face-to-face, especially if the interviewer has close connections with the course.

6 Case Studies

Collecting material to present case studies of individual students can bring an evaluation report to life. Statistics, percentages (even when enlivened by quotations, as they should be) accumulated by the methods described above, will often seem impersonal. A selection of case studies of a sample of students traces the experience of individuals. Readers can readily relate to a well-presented case study.

Case studies can be built up from individual interviews in which students are questioned about their motivation for coming on a course, their experience of learning whilst on it and the impact it is having/has had upon their lives. It can be supplemented, if wished, by samples of work and extracts from logs and diaries. Quotations from the interviews should be used to help readers understand the students' feelings and experiences. (**Appendix 11** is an example of one such case study.)

It is important to select samples carefully and explain to the reader how they were selected. You may wish to select a handful of students whose experiences can illustrate a particular point you wish to make; or students whose lives have been dramatically influenced by their learning. These studies, however, may not be representative of the total population of students on the course, and this should be made clear to readers. If you wish to select a representative sample, you should follow the guidelines on page 47 (Individual Interviews). Individual interviews may well provide the data from which you subsequently create case studies.

Advantages
i) Case studies make the most readable and interesting kind of report. Whether the readers are funders, inspectors, educationalists or the public makes little difference: almost everyone can readily identify with learning experiences as described in a case study and will be better able to understand an evaluation report if case studies are a part of it. The importance of producing a readable evaluation report must never be under-estimated. If a report is not read, it will not be acted upon!
ii) Student involvement in preparing a case study can and must be high. The student being studied, and her/his fellow students can all participate in collecting and selecting the material.
iii) A student who is being studied in this way may find her/his motivation considerably increased.

Disadvantages
i) Students selected for case studies can be 'set apart' from others – made to feel special and different. This may possibly prove harmful to the individual, or to fellow students not selected.
ii) Care must be taken to alter details which may make the students identifiable (if they wish to remain anonymous) and this can distort the true picture.

iii) If the sample is not representative, the studies may prove to be misleading.

iv) They can be very time-consuming to prepare.

7 Observation of Classes

Most teachers find it extremely uncomfortable to have someone watching them do their job and will often argue (with some truth) that the presence of another person in the room alters the interactions of the class members and teachers and makes the lesson very artificial. But if these barriers can be overcome, almost every teacher will find the feedback valuable.

Observation of classes is most useful if all staff involved in a course *first* discuss what makes a lesson work well or go badly and agree together an observation checklist. (**Appendix 12** is an example of the one devised by *Second Chance* staff. **Appendix 13** is a sample of a lesson observation checklist used on a teacher training course.) It is most helpful if colleagues can watch one another (rather than one person observe everyone else) as there is much to be learned about one's own teaching by observing others. Observations should take place at regular intervals, so that one lesson in isolation is not unrepresentative and so that staff and students can become accustomed to having an observer present. One week could be set aside each term for observation of teaching. In this way, observation becomes an integral part of a teacher's development. The frequency also reduces the awkwardness often felt by students and tutors.

Lessons should not be specially prepared by the teacher(s), otherwise the exercise becomes little more than a 'show', bearing little resemblance to normal classroom activity. Most teachers are only too well aware of how such 'shows' are prepared for Her Majesty's Inspectorate and how inaccurate the impressions conveyed may be (though a skilful and experienced H.M.I. is well aware of this). The purpose of an observation is not to pass a test or prove how good a teacher is. Rather, it is to obtain accurate information about everyday practices which can subsequently be discussed, leading to a better service.

The observation record can be presented to the teacher alone, or can (preferably) be discussed by a group of staff together so that difficulties as well as good practice can be shared. It is possible, and desirable, to involve students in these observations, discussing with them what should be looked for and asking them to play the role of observer from time to time.

Another alternative could be the use of a video recording of a lesson.

A video recording of a lesson.

If you decide to use video, it would be wise first to consult an expert or a book on video-making (such as **M.H. Taylor,** 1988). The education section of most good libraries will have numerous books to choose from.

Advantages
i) Insights are provided for each teacher into her/his strengths and weaknesses. A video recording would prove especially useful here.
ii) Staff can share both the difficulties of teaching and exchange good practice.

iii) There is a reduction of the isolation of teaching and an opportunity to offer and receive support.

iv) A continuous process of supervised 'in-service training' is established in which teachers can regularly examine their practice. This may well lead on to the provision of short courses exploring other teaching methods, use of audio-visual aids etc., if they are required.

Disadvantages
i) It can feel very threatening and nerve-racking and, as a result, an inaccurate impression may be gained. This can lead to a loss of self-confidence.

ii) The presence of an observer and/or a video-maker can lead to discomfort amongst students, too. Their enjoyment of a lesson may be impaired.

iii) Timetabling may make regular observation difficult to arrange.

8 & 9 Diaries, Log Books, Regular Evaluation Sheets

The methods described in the sections above are usually carried out relatively infrequently, possibly once per term. They can lack the detail and immediacy necessary to assist in the formulation of recommendations for change. There are other methods available which call for immediate evaluation or recording of a learning experience.

Both students and tutors can be asked to keep a regular diary of course activities and events and their responses to these. To write their diaries the students should be given as few guidelines as possible in order to allow spontaneous expression. One student may choose to focus upon course content; another upon relationships between students; others upon their own personal feelings. All are valid and will help to build a picture of the experience of learning. As these accounts may be quite personal reflections, you need to be sensitive about how to go about obtaining and using them.

A much more structured regular recording can be made instead of, or as well as, the diary. Session evaluation sheets (see **Appendix 14**) can be given out after each session, completed on the spot (they take only a few moments) and collected back in. Though superficial, they allow a tutor to tell instantly whether a particular session has been successful or not and so to remedy any problems in the next session.

A simple but very effective alternative to evaluation sheets can be used at the end of any session. Round off the session (or day or week) by asking each member of the group to name one thing they have enjoyed and one which they would change. As well as providing valuable information, this is a useful technique for ending a session, especially if the round of 'something I've enjoyed' comes last.

If regular evaluation techniques are to be used, it is vital that they are kept extremely brief. These three evaluation methods all share the common feature of being regular means of recording information whilst it is still 'alive'. The less frequent methods described earlier inevitably rely on longer-term memories and so many minor, but possibly significant, events tend to be submerged under a general impression.

Advantages
i) Small, but significant, variations are recorded.
ii) By collecting in and reading through the diaries and log books, a detailed picture of particular days/sessions can be built up.
iii) Diaries and log books can make fascinating reading and can be most valuable if re-read at a later date.
iv) Evaluation sheets allow immediate steps to be taken to rectify problems. They can, moreover, be accumulated to build up a picture of how parts of a course are being received by students.

Disadvantages
i) Like any other routine, a habit must be built up and this can be difficult to establish.
ii) Once established, responses can become dull, bland and routine due to the frequency of these methods. They may be completed without any real thought at all and may not be regularly analysed. Students and tutors may grow to resent using them.
iii) A large amount of material will be collected. Time must be available to use it fully, thereby demonstrating that it is valued, or else students and tutors will resent it and probably refuse to continue contributing. A good filing system is essential.

10 Course Records

Course records have provided the main source of data for the evaluation activities which have been carried out in recent years in adult and further education. The DES's 'efficiency indicators' produced in 'Managing Colleges Efficiently' (**DES/WO**, 1987) require that information be gathered about student numbers (staff/ student ratios), course completion rates, examination successes and students' destinations. These can provide a useful starting point for measuring the value of educational services. But their use is limited as they reveal only the extent to which one institution (or course) compares with others. They do not supply reasons for low or high effectiveness ratings. Nor do they ask the users to offer solutions to problems or recommendations for change.

Despite these shortcomings, and provided that they are used in conjunction with other methods described in this chapter, a wide range of records can be used to understand and illuminate a course. These could include minutes of meetings, samples of course work and materials, samples of students' work, photographs, etc. The kinds of information normally required by managers and funders all contribute to an evaluation. Records of numbers enrolling, attending and completing a course may well reflect upon its quality. The success levels of students in obtaining qualifications and their destinations on leaving (employment or access to further/higher education) can also contribute to the overall picture. But care must be taken when using these measures since the outcome they appear to indicate may be caused by many other factors. Many excellent courses may produce apparently poor results on these indicators. Nevertheless, provided that these quantitative measures are not simply taken at face value and questions are always asked about why students do or don't complete courses, pass examinations etc, they can be useful.

Advantages

i) Much of the data is already required and collected for managerial purposes. It just needs using.

ii) Records can offer a very good starting point for further enquiry. They can rapidly highlight outstanding successes or weak areas/ problems which need further investigation.

iii) Comparability between courses or between institutions (locally and nationally) can provide a useful 'yardstick' by which to assess a particular set of course records. Course records collected by nationally agreed criteria do offer such comparability.

Disadvantages
i) There is a great danger of over-simplistic interpretation leading to false conclusions. This is particularly dangerous when courses/services which are not alike are compared.
ii) It can lead to extra data collection without the data being used properly. The data can become an end in itself.
iii) There is a tendency in many people to believe figures, statistics, graphs etc, even though the method of collection may render them very inaccurate.
iv) People can convince themselves that they have already carried out a full evaluation once they have collected facts and figures and presented them in a report. The vital follow-up inquiries may never take place.

11 Informal Approaches

Information and impressions can be gathered in coffee breaks, over lunch, over a drink, from a chance encounter with students. Such approaches are rarely referred to as *methods* but they frequently provide 'leads': chance comments which can usefully be followed up more systematically in order to discover whether one student's casually offered opinion reflects a widely-held view. Quite often it does.

Confidentiality is crucial in these circumstances. It is most important that a student who makes a comment in a casual conversation does not suddenly discover that the topic is the centre of a major inquiry without any further consultation with her/him.

Advantages
i) Spontaneous comments are often very honest, coming 'straight from the heart' rather than formally articulated in an evaluation exercise.
ii) Students who volunteer comments rather than waiting for an evaluation activity, will often raise points which really matter to them. This may mean action can quickly be taken.
iii) All the snippets of information gathered informally over a period of time, together make a significant contribution to an evaluation.

iv) Highly significant comments may be made which may lead on to a full evaluation activity.

Disadvantages
i) By their very nature, informal comments are often subjective, selective and not very reliable or representative.
ii) A casually made comment may assume much greater importance than was intended by the speaker, or than it deserves.
iii) Student/tutor trust can be destroyed if informal comments are used or acted upon. Students may conclude that it is wiser to say nothing.
iv) Such comments are made in informal situations, are rarely recorded faithfully, if at all, and may be forgotten or distorted.

AT THE END
Group reviews, individual interviews and questionnaires are all suitable techniques to use at the end of the course. See the previous pages for more detail.

12 Testing Students
It may be appropriate on some courses to test the knowledge or skills acquired by students. There are courses in which testing is required (certificated courses, in particular). Such tests would reveal, to some extent, the effectiveness of the teaching. But they should not be unduly relied upon as a measure of teacher effectiveness (and they all too often are). Students who have been very badly taught may be highly motivated, work very hard outside the course, and score very well on tests. Conversely, external factors may cause students to do badly in tests despite having enjoyed successful learning experiences.

As one (relatively minor) evaluation tool, tests can be valuable, providing their conclusions are related to other evaluation information gained via group reviews, questionnaires etc. Course tutors should not introduce testing as an evaluation technique if it would not otherwise be appropriate, and staff and students should resist pressures to introduce testing if they are asked to do so by external agencies.

There is still a large body of somewhat ill-informed public opinion which believes that to evaluate the effectiveness of any teaching/ learning programme, students must be tested on entry and re-tested on completion of the course, and a comparison of the two will provide the evidence of success/failure and, thereby, of the quality of the service. This attitude is derived from research theory in the physical sciences where, for example, identical seed beds can be prepared. Plants are raised in identical conditions of heat/light, but doused with different fertilizers. The tests accurately reveal the relative effectiveness of the fertilizers. But students are not seeds from the same pod; learning environments are never identical seed beds, and education is not a dose of fertilizer. The weakness and unreliability of test techniques, moreover, make reliance on such testing extremely dangerous. **Derek Rowntree** (1987) describes the variety of test techniques available, with their limitations (and uses). Anyone contemplating the use of tests would do well to first read his book.

Advantages
i) If testing is already a part of course procedures, it would seem foolish to ignore a source of important data which is readily available.
ii) Assessing students' knowledge, skills etc. after a period of learning is an important way of measuring what is sometimes referred to as 'value-added'. It is one measure of the value of a course.
iii) Excessively good or poor results (as compared to other groups, other institutions, national averages and/or previous years' results) do require closer examination and inquiry into the causes.

Disadvantages
i) Tests can assume much too great importance.
ii) Those courses which can demonstrate that learning has taken place by measuring students' development through tests may be given greater status than those which cannot present impressive figures.
iii) Tests may be pressed upon students where they are not appropriate to the course, in order to provide quotable statistics.
iv) Tests are not nearly as reliable as most people think they are. Most have serious weaknesses and shortcomings as a way of measuring educational growth.

13 Displays of Work
For many courses, especially craft courses, an end-of-course display would be an appropriate method to *contribute* to the evaluation. If the

goal of the course is to produce something (cake-decoration, woodwork, artwork, a play), then a display of the product is a clear indication of the level of success.

Advantages
i) Displays and performances can motivate students and give them great pride and satisfaction in their achievements.
ii) "a picture speaks a thousand words".

Disadvantages
i) Working for the display or performance can dominate the learning process and distort it.
ii) Sometimes only the 'best' work is displayed. This is unrepresentative as a method of evaluation, and can be very damaging to any student whose work is omitted.
iii) Because in a display or performance only the end product of learning is seen, no judgement can be made of the process of learning or of student satisfaction etc.

AFTER THE COURSE ENDS

Sometimes it is months or years before the value of an educational experience can be properly assessed. An evaluation should, therefore, contain some procedures for carrying out follow-up enquiries. These can be relatively simple studies of students' destinations (jobs, further education courses etc.) or much more complex and detailed enquiries in which students are asked to carefully assess their learning experience.

Most of the techniques described in this chapter could be considered for use. A questionnaire is likely to be most suitable for large-scale courses where possibly hundreds of students may need to be contacted. With smaller learning groups, a reunion meeting could be both enjoyable and practical.

The results of follow-up studies are much more liable to be biased. Re-union meetings, for example, tend to be occasions for 'bonhomie' and rose-tinted memories and it can be hard to elicit an accurate picture. Those who return will usually be those who were most satisfied and who want to see fellow students and staff. Questionnaires can have a similar response, though often less extreme. Most of those who take the trouble to respond to a questionnaire, perhaps several years later, do so because the course has had some major impact upon them. This must be borne in mind when such evaluation takes place, especially if the response rate is low (and it is usually very low).

Despite these shortcomings, post-course evaluation is important and attempts to carry it out are worth the effort. On *Second Chance* a large scale post-course evaluation was carried out by a group of about ten students over three months. They worked closely with me, designing and carrying out the evaluation. The results of our inquiries can be read in **J. Edwards,** 1986 (Chapter 10). The experience of carrying out this evaluation was a very enjoyable one and I believe that because students devised the questions and carried out the interviewing, the results were more accurate than they could possibly have been if I had worked alone. The exercise was, moreover, a valuable learning experience for the students involved, as they acquired research techniques and experience.

Conclusion

The wide range of methods which have been described in these pages have all been drawn from evaluations which have taken place. They have all been tried and tested and found useful. Some adaptations would be needed for use in the youth and community service, amongst voluntary groups, etc. But the starting point – clarifying the goals of all those involved – remains the same. Minor adaptations of methodology would then follow relatively easily.

These methods all involve student participation. This is deliberate and is based on the belief that an evaluation should make the service accountable first and foremost to its users.

Reference was made earlier to the Workers' Educational Association's system of student management via its Branches. In a conference in 1985 they formulated a checklist of methods of class evaluation (**Appendix 15**) which provides an insight into how a national educational association with 178,000 members has co-ordinated its evaluation procedures. The ideas in this appendix could prove useful to other organisations/institutions.

Chapter 3

If after reading this chapter you feel overwhelmed, remember it is up to you, in consultation with others, to decide what should be evaluated and select from these various approaches any which will help you. A modest beginning may lead to additional time and resources being allocated to enable you to undertake a fuller evaluation. If this does not happen, whatever information you are able to uncover will help to improve the quality of the course and your own and your students' satisfaction.

CHAPTER 4

Problems and solutions

Introduction

It would be misleading to suggest that evaluation brings nothing but good. However well-intentioned and skilful the organisers of an evaluation may be, problems are likely to arise. Some understanding of them in advance can help with their solution. This chapter examines some of the problems which most frequently occur. Some are mainly practical (e.g. extension of teachers' workloads, and coping with the data produced) and can be resolved in advance to everyone's satisfaction. Others, though, are concerned with the emotional reactions of staff and students to evaluation. It may be impossible to resolve them fully, but it is essential to recognise the validity of these reactions and create opportunities for them to be discussed. Mutual understanding and empathy can help a great deal. The chapter concludes by asking (and, hopefully, answering) the question, *"Is it worth it?"*

The 'threat'

The purpose of an evaluation is to improve the quality of services. If the evaluation were to reveal standards and practices which are not acceptable to those with the power to fund/employ, the result may be closure, disciplinary action, even dismissal. These possible outcomes, though rare, should not be ignored. Many staff who participate in an evaluation are initially suspicious of its purposes and only too well aware of the possibility of these outcomes. There will be differences of opinion between participants regarding at what point it becomes right to reveal information which may lead to these consequences. The responsibility for taking these decisions ought to be shared amongst the steering group or its equivalent. (See **Chapters 2** and **5** for further information.)

Happily such extreme outcomes are exceptional. Nevertheless, evaluation usually brings discomfort and feelings of anxiety for a number of reasons. Old hierarchies are disturbed: students evaluate teachers; teachers evaluate managers. Those people who are accustomed only to being answerable to those 'above' now find their ideas and practices open to scrutiny and sometimes to criticism. A *Second Chance* tutor described it like this:

> *"It's a challenge and a threat. Automatically most of us feel like it's a threat. Like councillors and doctors we want to be trusted, not questioned. We teachers like to think we're more liberal than doctors etc. but really we're not. Evaluation allows all our assumptions to be challenged. It's a major challenge being evaluated."*

It's a major challenge being evaluated.

Coping with criticism can be hard, especially for the unconfident or inexperienced teacher. There are no easy answers, but there are many ways to make it easier.

Positive feedback should always be given before negative comments are made. It is always easier to examine our weaknesses after our confidence has been raised by hearing about what we do well. The phrasing of evaluation questions is important. Instead of asking, *"What was good/bad?"*, you can ask, *"What have you learned from this?"* and *"What might be improved or changed?"*

As far as possible, staff whose work is to be commented upon should be involved in self-evaluation first, so that they may to some extent be prepared for what they hear. Try to create the kind of atmosphere in which staff feel they 'own' the evaluation and in which they can value comments as useful information rather than criticism. In this climate 'failures' and 'mistakes' can be seen as a healthy, normal part of everyone's learning (including a teacher's) and as an opportunity to put things right. Always seek solutions – concrete, practical ones – so that no one goes away feeling hopeless. Set time aside to discuss how people *feel* about the evaluation. This needs to be openly discussed, because if they begin to feel negative, hostile or despondent, little good will come of the exercise.

Consult fully all those likely to be involved. Discuss with them who will have access to what information and whether individuals will be identified in any way. Ensure there is a regular forum where anxieties or queries can be raised and taken seriously. Provide prompt and regular reports of the information gathered. Be scrupulous about confidentiality – never succumbing to the temptation to pass on interesting bits of information which fall outside the agreements about what can be revealed.

If evaluation is undertaken by one group of staff it can frequently have an impact upon others not directly involved in it. If, for example, in a college of further education, one group of staff decide to undertake evaluation of their work, other staff may become angry, feeling that this is 'forcing their hand' as their students will expect it, too. The subtle changes in hierarchy and expectation can spread amongst the student body creating repercussions in other courses. This is not a reason for drawing back, but it does demonstrate how important it is to discuss fully what you are planning to do, beforehand, with others who are not directly implicated in it.

Conversely, students who are generally not very satisfied with the quality of the service they receive may use the newly-acquired opportunities in an evaluation to heap all kinds of criticism upon the heads of those few who choose to expose themselves to it. Because there is no other channel, and because anger and frustration have not been expressed on other courses, students may focus all their criticism upon the tutors who ask for their opinions. This can be a painful experience, and a galling one if other staff appear to be continuing their practices unchallenged and unchanging.

We can see that there are many good reasons why teachers (and any other staff involved in an evaluation) may experience feelings of anxiety, whether these are well-founded or not. Steps can and should be taken to reduce feelings of threat. Sensitivity is always needed. By taking these steps you will go a long way towards minimising the anxieties and will thereby improve the likelihood of the whole process being productive. But recognise that after all this has been done, a threat will still exist, and it cannot be eradicated.

Tensions

In any group there will be differences in approach, even clearly differing philosophies. During an evaluation, these differences become much more openly articulated as colleagues and students explore goals and methods. If, at the same time, difficulties experienced by staff are becoming more public through evaluation data, this can lead to tensions between colleagues or between staff and students. Whilst evaluation is most unlikely to damage good relationships, it can certainly exacerbate problems in poor ones. Care needs to be taken in dealing with these tensions. Differences can release creative energy through constructive debate, but the defending of entrenched positions is damaging and destructive. If attention has been paid to group dynamics at the outset (as was earlier recommended), it will pay off in these potentially difficult situations.

Workloads/time

Extra work will obviously be involved. Observing classes, keeping diaries or logbooks, constructing and analysing questionnaires and presenting a written report, organising group reviews or individual interviewing – every one of these and other processes requires a time commitment from teachers and students. Paperwork can increase dramatically and few welcome such a move.

But evaluation is part of the teaching/learning cycle.

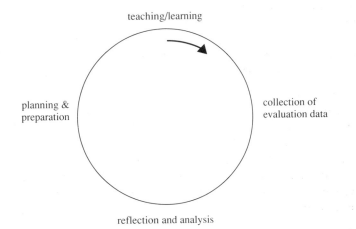

teaching/learning

planning & preparation

collection of evaluation data

reflection and analysis

Planning and preparation for teaching have long been recognised to be part of the teacher's professional responsibility and unions have won the right for paid time to be allocated for these activities. The last part of the cycle – full evaluation, not just the marking of students' work – now needs to be awarded the same recognition both by teachers themselves (and their unions) and also by employers, who must be urged to allocate paid time for these activities. Changes such as these are likely to be achieved slowly. In the meantime, it is up to each person or group when making proposals for new courses, to cost in evaluation time. Those in existing courses should argue the case as persuasively as they can. *It is worth noting that in industry approximately 10% of the retail price of a product is invested in quality control.*

Some of the activities described in this book are simply 'good practice' and should be part of any good teacher's way of working. So, if time cannot be won immediately, think about what you could do to evaluate your work.

We must not forget students' time: equally valuable. Evaluation will require some of that time being used which would usually be occupied in other ways. Students will need to appreciate the value of the activities, for themselves and for others, if they are to willingly engage in them and participate fully. This can be achieved in a number of ways. Introduce the concept of evaluation to them at the same time as the course is explained/introduced. From the outset they can then see evaluation as a part of normal learning activities.

Students should be fully involved in deciding what should be examined, so that issues which are important to them are on the agenda. This could be achieved by student representation on a steering group, or by regular consultation with student groups. They should be able to see how a particular activity will help them either directly (by leading to immediate changes, perhaps) or indirectly (by improving their capacity to understand how they learn best).

Evaluation should not be left until the end of the course, otherwise students cannot benefit greatly. Most students, provided they have been listened to and consulted throughout a course, are happy to participate in a final evaluation at the end of a course, or post-course activities. They recognise that others will benefit after them.

Coping with the data

It is easy to be over-ambitious, with the result that you may soon be floundering under mountains of paper, tapes, etc. You may find that you cannot possibly analyse it all. This means that having sought information and opinions, you ignore them. This will leave those who offered you their time and thoughts feeling angry and frustrated. You may succeed in analysing everything (possibly at the expense of free time or by deferring other important tasks) and produce so many reports that there is no opportunity for each to be fully considered.

When you and/or an evaluation steering group decide what to explore at the outset, you must also consider how and by whom the data will be analysed and, equally important, how, when and by whom the reports will be considered. You must then prioritize your activities in the light of the amount of time available to carry out a particular task (**Appendix 4** can guide you through this process). A realistic assessment must be made of how much time a task will take (pilot studies can help you make these judgements). You can be sure that you will underestimate the time required. Being over-ambitious kills everyone's enthusiasm eventually. It is far better to start small, do something really well, and gradually build up.

You will also need to devise an effective storage and filing system if you are to prevent valuable information being lost or taking so much time to retrieve that it is easier to ignore it.

Honesty

Many of us find it very hard to offer or take criticism in a constructive way. We find it hard to differentiate between criticising a particular action and criticising the person who performed it. Students and teachers need to

Many of us find it very hard to take criticism in a constructive way.

learn how to give frank opinions in a positive way. Otherwise it will be done aggressively or, more likely, people will prefer to say nothing. They will often say nothing openly, but will continue to pass critical comments to one another – not to the person concerned.

Sometimes, if relationships between colleagues or between students and staff are good, and if there is a high degree of satisfaction with the service overall, it can be even harder to obtain honest criticism. Students may be afraid of upsetting their teachers over relatively trivial points – afraid of seeming petty-minded.

The best way to overcome this difficulty is to talk openly about evaluation and explain how it will help the staff as well as students. Emphasise that teachers, like students, want to get better at what they do and that learning and improving is a lifelong process. Make it clear that criticism is necessary. Give students an opportunity to offer praise as well – a necessary counter-balance.

Finally, when criticism is offered, don't become angry or defensive. If you do find it upsetting, you can acknowledge this, explaining that it can hurt to hear criticism but that you still need and value it. Everyone recognises this feeling.

Provided you begin evaluation processes early on in a course, and if you are honest with students, these difficulties should diminish quite rapidly and you will be rewarded with reasonably honest replies to questions which will help you understand your own teaching. You will then have the satisfaction of getting better at your work.

But it is essential to keep one question at the forefront of your mind throughout all evaluation processes, *"Did they tell me the truth?"*

Interpretation

Value-judgements lie at the heart of evaluation. Interpreting very different statements can prove extremely difficult. Whatever methods you choose to use, one thing can be guaranteed: you will hear opposing views. It could not be otherwise. What suits one student perfectly will be completely useless for another and every student will be somewhere on a continuum between these two extremes. One individual's judgement of the value of a particular learning experience may alter dramatically over time. Something which appears to be confusing, time-wasting or unnecessary immediately after it has been studied or learned, could be judged to be of enormous importance by the same student at a later date. Or vice-versa.

Managers may hold a different view of what is important from teachers and/or students. Neither managers nor teachers are homogeneous groups and, like students, their judgements will vary greatly.

Faced with such conflicting data, what is an evaluator to do? There could be a temptation to abandon it all. What is the use of spending large amounts of time (and money, perhaps) if an agreed conclusion cannot, by definition, be achieved?

There is, of course, no easy answer to this question. The starting point, though, is the recognition that it is a problem. This may appear obvious but there are individuals who believe they have found 'the truth'. Such people are, at the very least, misguided – at worst, dangerously misleading.

Several solutions present themselves which together can help us to deal with the problem. Include as many people as possible in the process of interpreting data. This can help overcome the tendency of any individual to see what she/he wants or expects to see. When reporting data, it is essential for an evaluator to include the range of views. Bland generalisations about 'the majority' can mask vitally important individual differences in responses. For example, after introducing a new element in a course, an evaluation may reveal no overall change in the percentage of satisfied students. This could mask the fact that younger students who have left school relatively recently respond very well to the change, whilst older students respond very badly. Averaged out, this could equal no change. But within it there are very significant differences in response.

Much evaluation throws up more new questions than answers. Further evaluation is often required in order to answer these. In this way our understanding of students' learning and responses grows.

It is important to be unafraid of encountering conflicting views, to recognise the complexity of human responses to learning, to seek to represent these faithfully, leaving readers of reports to add their own interpretation. Gradually patterns and trends do emerge and can be identified as such, but there can never be a universal truth.

Communicating clearly

Clear and appropriate communication is essential at every stage of an evaluation. In the early stages of deciding what to evaluate, ambiguities can easily arise. At the outset, participants often have a very different interpretation of the word 'evaluation' and its relationship to monitoring and management information systems. It is worth spending time ensuring that there is a shared common understanding of the concepts. Much of the resistance to evaluation occurs because of misunderstanding and failure to communicate.

The writing of clear, unambiguous questions proves difficult at all times and many a questionnaire has been spoiled because students have interpreted particular questions in many different ways. You should seek advice on how to write questionnaires (see **Appendix 7**) and try out a pilot study first to see which questions prove to be ambiguous.

Deciding how to communicate evaluation data in reports must be very carefully considered. All too often a report is ignored partly because its format and language is inappropriate to its audience. It is important to consider just who will read a report and what their areas of interest and concern are likely to be. An evaluation report offers the opportunity to focus attention upon strengths and weaknesses of a service. If it is to be considered by decision-makers (and it should be if the evaluation is to have an impact), a clear set of recommendations needs to be presented. Lengthy reports are less likely to be read by busy people than brief, succinct ones. It is tempting to include everything you have discovered, but this is likely to be counter-productive. That cherished additional information could always be presented in appendices for the interested reader.

In the pages above are described some of the major difficulties encountered by staff and students undertaking evaluation work. By anticipating them and by working out in advance how to deal with them, most can be overcome. The chances of finding solutions are much greater when a representative steering group meets regularly.

Is it worth it?

On *Second Chance* an assessment of the effects of evaluation demonstrated very clearly that the time and effort had been worthwhile. So much so, that the evaluation, which was originally conceived of as a short-term, 'one-off' research exercise, became part of everyday working procedures. The comments of the tutors quoted below have been echoed by many other teachers and organisers with whom I have spent time in many different parts of the country.

All but one of the *Second Chance* tutors were pleasantly surprised by the effects the evaluation had upon themselves and the course. It brought a clearer sense of direction, improved their ability to teach, which in turn brought greater job satisfaction. It reduced the isolation that, even within a closely-knit team, they had experienced. It gave most team members a greater degree of involvement in course organisation and more responsibility for the project as a whole. Whilst it could not be proved that evaluation alone created these changes, the tutors believe that some would never have occurred, and others would have happened much more slowly without it. A few of the tutors' comments, quoted from taped individual interviews, convey their enthusiasm:

> "I'm now clearer about what it is I want to achieve; and not only what, but how I want to achieve it."

> "It made everybody more conscious of how they teach, what they teach, whether it is what they ought to be teaching and how effective the teaching is. One of the problems of teaching is that as long as you think you are getting over what you want to get over, that's all there is to it. Whether people are actually picking up the bits and pieces is their problem, not yours. Evaluation brought us to notice that the other part of the equation – finding out what students learn – is part of teaching."

> "I didn't realise the evaluation would play such a part in the day-to-day running and teaching of the course. It has been totally different from what I expected. It's involved me a great deal and that's good because it's given me a structure and clearer aims. It gave me a chance to discover things that were, perhaps, in the back of my mind already. And it's given us badly needed practical help."

"Evaluation has changed my ideas about there being two groups: the educators and those being educated. It's made me rethink all of that."

"Evaluation answered some questions that had been hanging about in my head but I'd never had the time to find out, except by unsatisfactory 'straw-polls'. If you want to be a better teacher, you're bound to find it useful."

"It's emphasised the point that good educational practice is a skill which can be acquired – that it's not just a matter of charisma. That's led us to feel we can make a worthwhile contribution."

"Part of the problem of teaching is the loneliness. Evaluation helped because it lessened the isolation. We could talk about it. But it was very important that you, as the evaluator, were part of the course, not a distant outsider, and generally sympathetic to it."

Just as the tutors were changed by the process, so was the course – in most tutors' view for the better:

"We dumped a lot of romantic notions (for example, the belief that it will all come from the students) that bedevilled the early days. Constant assessments of how the course is going, the agonising, even the rows, have all helped enormously. It's much more satisfactory now, I'm in no doubt at all. The research and evaluation have made a great improvement to teaching."

"We've all become much more conscious that we are teachers. We used to discuss the notes at length, what they said, without wondering whether they were useful and intelligible to students. That's changed a lot. There's a greater awareness of what students actually expected and wanted, and comparing that with what tutors wanted. Everyone is better informed now."

Were the evaluation processes equally valuable to the students? It is harder to ascertain this. Students were able to clearly describe their experience of learning on the course and the impact it had upon them. But they were not easily able to identify how significant a part the evaluation processes played in their experience of learning on the course.

It can be said with certainty that almost all students welcomed the part they could play in evaluating the course and making recommendations. They took it very seriously and participated fully and helpfully. They soon grew accustomed to the changed relationship with tutors, where they, the learners, were considered to have a valid opinion about their learning and the tutors' teaching. This had a powerful impact upon their view of themselves vis-a-vis 'professionals' in general. They began to see professionals as people who were paid to provide/offer a service to them, and when that service was inadequate, they had a right to expect and require something better. (An example of this can be found in the case study in **Appendix 11.**)

There have been a number of occasions when former *Second Chance* students have gone on to other courses elsewhere in the city and found them wanting. Instead of tolerating it or leaving, on several occasions students have taken action which was directly based upon their experience as evaluators. They have been able to define precisely what was wrong (because they had become accustomed to analysing learning and teaching) and suggest solutions. With the confidence this gave them, they have gone on to talk with other students on their new courses, called meetings with the staff concerned and put their comments and recommendations to them. The outcomes of such action have almost always been beneficial, though it must be said that some of the staff concerned initially found it very hard to accept this forthright approach. In some colleges small-scale evaluation procedures have been introduced, directly arising from the former *Second Chance* students' suggestions. In others, much more satisfactory consultation procedures have been adopted.

All of the students who have been involved in creating these changes in other colleges and institutions state unequivocally that they would not have dreamed of taking such steps, let alone known how to go about it successfully, had it not been for the experience and resulting confidence they gained from participating regularly in evaluation.

From time to time, small groups of students have played a much more active role in evaluation procedures. They have been responsible for designing questionnaires, carrying out interviews, analysing the data, formulating conclusions and recommendations. One such group explored the impact of the course upon students' lives using post-course follow up

(**J. Edwards,** 1986, Chapter 10). Another examined why students leave before completing the course. One group worked on a study of the difficulties encountered by adults who work and try to obtain day-release to attend classes. The data they produced was used in a chapter of a book about paid educational leave. (**J. Mace & M. Yarnit** (eds), 1987, Chapter 9). All of these groups of students have worked voluntarily and enthusiastically. They have had the opportunity to acquire research skills and the satisfaction of discovering information which could be of use to others. These research activities have been an extension of the evaluation procedures to which they had become accustomed.

From the point of view of tutors and students alike the answer to the question *"Is it worth it?"* would in almost every case be *"Yes"*. But evaluation in isolation will not create major changes. Much information will emerge. How effectively it will be *used* depends not least upon the managers.

How effectively it will be used depends not least upon the managers.

These managers may be the practitioners themselves, in some circumstances, or they may be external. Good managers will use the information which emerges to build upon strengths and find solutions to problems. Poor managers will either ignore it all and carry on regardless, or abuse their access to the information.

This leads us to the issue of access to data and certain other matters which must be considered by steering groups before evaluation takes place. These and other important issues are discussed in the next chapter.

CHAPTER 5

Some key issues to consider before and during evaluation

I hope it is by now clear that if a group of people decide together to evaluate their service, their chances of doing this successfully and avoiding major problems will be far greater if they establish a steering group which should consider a number of key issues. These issues need full discussion *before* the work begins. They should be reviewed on a regular basis.

Some of the issues which I have discovered are important to discuss and resolve are listed below. There are others which could have been included and new ones emerge all the time. This is why the steering group needs to meet regularly and keep these matters under review.

Accountability and control

> *"The evaluation process is just a tool to be used – and how it is used will depend upon the people who control the process."*
> **M. Q. Patton** (1981)

Be clear at the outset who will control the evaluation because whoever does so will have the authority to decide all the other issues e.g. what will be evaluated, by whom, how, with what resources, and so on. *Ideally, control should belong to a broadly-based evaluation committee or steering group representing all those who will be involved,* rather than (as is traditional) managers or those in authority.

Ideally, teachers and, perhaps, students should form the majority of a steering group, and union representatives should also be invited to participate. *This helps to establish the evaluation in a positive atmosphere* – one where the views of those who deliver and use the services are seen as paramount. Staff and students are then more likely to believe in evaluation as a means of improving the quality of a service, rather than as an instrument to expose or damage them.

Control is probably the most fundamental issue to discuss and decide upon. If the wrong decision is taken, workers and their unions will be likely to see it as yet another management device to be resisted at all costs.

Purpose

Is the purpose of evaluation to improve the quality of the services; to allow managers to take decisions about expansion or reduction of services; to share information about good practice and failure with a wider (perhaps national) audience; to break down hierarchies in establishments? It may be a combination of these and other purposes which you have in mind.

Care must be taken to ensure these various purposes are not confused. Some are incompatible. If managers wish to use the evaluation as a 'quality control' exercise, this would mean that certain forms of measurement would be introduced. Staff would naturally be apprehensive and likely to attempt to defend themselves and their services. Students would probably collude in this defence. Information may then be hidden and distorted. Whereas, if none of the data were to be made available to managers because the evaluation was seen as a means of staff development (thereby leading to improved quality), a very different result would probably be generated, with a great deal more honesty and usefulness.

The purpose of the evaluation, therefore, needs full discussion and clear decisions at the outset. It should be open to amendment and change by the evaluation steering group or committee if/when the need arises.

Linking evaluation to existing systems

Within most institutions there are already numerous systems for collecting information. These are sometimes collectively referred to as

Management Information Systems (MIS) and may include data on student enrolments, attendances, completion of courses, withdrawals, examination results, destinations etc. The extent of this data collection is rapidly increasing and frequently causes frustration and irritation to teachers and students alike who may not fully understand the reasons why it is collected or the use to which it will be put.

If evaluation is introduced without careful linking to existing information systems, there will be great (and justified) resistance. It will be seen as yet another task – worse still, a duplication of data. One of the early jobs of any steering group must be to examine all the existing data collection systems and find ways of utilising these in evaluation plans and activities. A subsequent and equally valuable task could be to evaluate the impact and effectiveness of the institution's data collection system.

A steering group could also examine the existing management structure of the institution in order to decide how it can be most effective in ensuring that evaluation reports are considered by appropriate bodies and recommendations acted upon. A complete review of the management structure may also prove worthwhile.

Access to information

Everyone, (managers, staff and students) must know exactly who will have access to what kinds of information and how any changes in such agreements may be made. Confidentiality and anonymity must be part of early discussions on access to information. Whatever is agreed should preferably be written down to avoid ambiguity and possible disputes at a later date. Mutual trust is essential. It cannot be built up if participants fear that information may be casually passed on without their permission having been sought.

Initially at least, evaluation works best if those people whose work is to be evaluated can take the decisions about what should be reported, how it should be reported and to whom. Such decisions could be reached by groups of teachers and students in conjunction with the steering group and managers. This control over access to information is, of course, open to abuse, but no more so than the abuse which could be made by managers of their access to information.

The issue is clearly a delicate one and will inevitably arise frequently throughout any evaluation. There are no ready solutions, and decisions about access to information may need to be altered from time to time. This should be done only after reviewing the evaluation (which must be done on a regular basis). *Remember that successful evaluation requires mutual trust* and, as most of the power in any institution lies in the hands of its managers, reversing this trend and placing some power in the hands of staff and students can help to build the necessary trust.

Value-judgements and the criteria for success

It is the responsibility of those who carry out evaluation procedures to collect, analyse and report information as objectively as they are able. Whilst carrying out these steps they must endeavour to avoid bias. Every effort should be made to present an account which is as representative as possible of the views of different parties involved. They must be able to feel that their views have been fairly and openly put and that the findings are honest and impartial. Judgement about what is worthwhile and what is wrong should be made by the readers of the reports and by those who have responsibility for ensuring that action is taken.

Nevertheless, value-judgements lie at the heart of all evaluation. Decisions about what should be evaluated and what constitutes 'success' in any environment involve value-judgements. This is why no one individual should be responsible for making such judgements and decisions should be taken jointly with members of an evaluation steering group. The criteria upon which judgements will be made should be jointly agreed and written down.

Implementing changes

Successful evaluation depends upon a commitment to change whenever it is possible to do so. Without this commitment, the process is time-wasting and extremely frustrating to all who are involved.

If the required changes cannot be made, or must be postponed, full discussion of the reasons for this is essential. It should be made clear at the outset that not every recommendation can or will be implemented straight away, and what mechanisms exist for taking these decisions.

Staff and students should always be encouraged to make clear recommendations for changes. Although they may not have sufficient information to know whether these recommendations can be implemented, they have much the best understanding of teaching/ learning processes.

Resources

As we have seen earlier, resources will affect many of the decisions to be taken. Costs in terms of time and material resources for evaluation must be counted. It would be very inefficient if time was allowed for these processes to take place, but no money made available to write up and reproduce reports, so that the experiences and understanding gained could not be shared.

Despite the stringent financial controls and, in many cases, cutbacks in the funding of further and adult education, a convincing case can and must be made for adequate resources. With massive changes taking place, there is an urgent need for good evaluation data to assist decision-making. This is now being recognised. The financial implications for implementing the FEU's 1989 recommendations in **Towards an Educational Audit,** or for applying for the BS5750 are considerable. (See **Introduction** pp. 3 to 6.) Large sums of money would be required to undertake all this. In any sizeable institution several posts would need to be created or redirected. *Local authorities and other funding bodies must be pressed to properly fund evaluation.* Full-time permanent posts are needed to ensure co-ordination of activities throughout their areas and to provide staff training. Time must be allocated for the work within colleges and other institutions.

National and local networks are needed to effectively spread the knowledge gained. Reports, working groups, conferences, courses, etc. could all be part of such networks.

Resource banks with samples of evaluation procedures – undertaken locally and nationally – would help newcomers get started, until they develop the confidence and experience to devise their own 'tools'.

Finally, if a representative steering group or committee is established to consider issues such as those outlined above, major problems will be avoided. A useful, feasible evaluation exercise should be able to proceed with maximum co-operation. Without such a committee, if decisions of this magnitude are taken, it is most unlikely that co-operation will be achieved and the potential benefits of evaluation are likely to be lost.

CHAPTER 6

Training for evaluation

Although much of what has been described in this guide is common-sense, training should play a key part in preparation for evaluation. Training can take place in a localised way, with workers and students from a particular course or project coming together to participate in training. The role of students in the training process should be carefully considered. When the training takes place at local level, it is relatively easy to include either all the students or representatives of students in training groups. When training takes place at an institutional or city-wide level, it can prove more difficult to work out the role of students and decide who should attend training sessions. The W.E.A. resolves this through its 'Branch' structure of organisation and involves students in management and training. (The document reproduced in **Appendix 15** was devised by workers and students attending a training conference.)

The training format in this chapter has been developed over numerous training sessions and may provide a useful model from which to work.

Suggested Training Format
The following format comprises two introductory sessions, each lasting $2^1/_2$ to 3 hours, combined, if possible, in a single training day. Optimum numbers vary, but about 15 to 20 works well. Groups can be convened who work in broadly similar work areas or brought together from a variety of different services. I have found that in the initial stages it works better to separately train people from different fields of work e.g. youth workers, adult basic education workers, volunteer literacy tutors or teachers who are following an externally set syllabus

such as G.C.S.E. Too many combinations can prove very confusing initially, though the cross-fertilisation of ideas can be most useful once people have some experience of evaluation.

It is helpful if someone can attend the training sessions as a notetaker. Many of the points raised in the plenary discussions will need to be taken up in subsequent 'in-service' training sessions. They may be forgotten if notes are not taken.

N.B. Staff attending initial evaluation training sessions always have numerous questions they want to have answered and anxieties which need discussing. There must be sufficient flexibility in the training format to allow time for these discussions. If staff feel anxious they cannot learn. A set of questions (such as those in **Appendix 16**) can be circulated in advance. They could also be returned in advance to allow prior consideration by trainers.

Session 1 (a.m.)

1. What is evaluation? How we currently evaluate our work and why (45 min.)

a) A short discussion amongst the whole group to define the term 'evaluation' and discuss how they feel about it.
e.g. "What does the word 'evaluation' mean to you?"

b) Small groups (of 4 to 6 members each) discuss their current evaluation procedures. Discussions can be focussed around a set of questions such as those in **Appendices 17, 18, 19, or 20.** *This session will be more successful if copies are sent to participants in advance.*

c) Plenary session with brief group report-backs **(45 min.)** *with lists drawn up of*
i) current practices
ii) problems encountered
iii) reasons for evaluating

---

2. What do you want to find out about? (1 hour)

a) 10 minutes quiet time for each course member to write a list of all the issues/problems/concerns (however big or small) they can think of which they would like to investigate. (Work sheets in **Appendix 4** *may prove useful here.)*

or

b) An alternative way of working is to ask people to work in pairs. Each can draw up an individual list but the stimulus of working with a partner can produce more ideas.

c) Plenary session. Ask each person to give one idea. Go round the group. If time permits, another idea can be drawn from each person. Encourage course members to add any new ideas to their own lists which might prove relevant.

LUNCH BREAK

Session 2 (p.m.)

1. How should we do it? Methods (1 hour)
This session concentrates upon considering the possible methods (outlined in this guide) which could be used.

a) It could take the form of a lecture and subsequent discussion, if there is someone available in your area who has experience of evaluating courses/services. If so, the full group should remain together, though it is also useful for participants to spend some time in small groups to consider the suitability of various methods (as suggested in (b) below).

b) Small groups (of 5 or 6) could discuss together the methods outlined in this guide and consider which would be most appropriate.

---

2. How to get started? (1 hour)
A wide-ranging plenary discussion could cover the following areas:

a) securing time/resources

b) establishing an evaluation committee/steering group

c) how to select priorities

d) further training needs for course members and others

e) action planning – ideally each person should leave with a concrete plan of action. It's a good idea to pause before the end and get everyone to write down the next step they are going to take and the date by which they will take it. Ideas could then be shared amongst the group.

*Planning sheets (as in **Appendix 4**) could be distributed and a short discussion about how to use them could follow.*

3. Problems/worries (1 hour)
Time should be spent in discussion of any problems or anxieties which have not been raised or fully discussed earlier in the day. Some of these will need to be raised in steering group meetings and/or with managers.

If the training sessions work well, the outcome will almost certainly be a request for future training meetings. The frequency and purpose of these meetings must be decided locally, but if follow-up meetings are to take place immediately, then the planning sheets in **Appendix 4** could be used there.

Sometimes an individual will want to return to their place of work or learning and discuss evaluation with others and take decisions with them about what is to happen. Then subsequent training sessions of a practical kind could take place in which small groups of people with common areas of interest can work together on writing questionnaires, planning reviews, etc. After another period of time, when the 'tools' have been tried out, the groups can meet again to talk about how they got on and continue with planning and specific training. They can also devise systems for creating resource banks of evaluation activities which can be referred to on future occasions to economise on time and effort and to share good ideas. These suggested training sessions are designed to get the processes of evaluation started. Further training should be budgeted for. All subsequent training should be as practical as possible, and it too should be evaluated.

When an institution is being evaluated, managers will also need to participate in training sessions since they will be actively included in evaluation themselves as well as being called upon to support the work of their staff. Training for managers could be combined with training for teaching staff. It is usually preferable, though, to hold initial training sessions separately. Some joint training sessions may prove valuable at a later stage. Training for managers can successfully follow a similar format to that outlined in this chapter.

CHAPTER 7

Conclusion

The pace of change is accelerating. This is as true in the field of education as it is in new technology. Some of us find this exhilarating, exciting: we welcome these changes. Most of us find it confusing, unsettling, even frightening. How can we know if the changes that are being largely thrust upon us are truly beneficial? How can we judge their worth in advance and after they have been implemented? How can we enter into the process of creating change rather than reacting, often negatively, to it? There has never been a greater need for evaluation than there is now. With increased competitiveness, *the quality of the services offered has never mattered more.* There is an urgent need for accurate information to assist us in making judgements about proposed changes. There is an equally urgent need for information, for rapid feedback, as new innovations are put to the test. They are bound to need modifying. Systematic evaluation can supply the information to assist the processes of change.

Evaluation can and does take place at several different levels, always yielding valuable information. We evaluate, at an almost unconscious level, everything we do. In a classroom, a teacher responds to students' facial expressions, comments, answers, etc. and makes appropriate adjustments. At the end of a lesson we may automatically find ourselves reflecting upon how it went, and this will help us plan subsequent lessons. But we can formalise this process, make it more deliberate and fruitful by asking our students to evaluate the lesson verbally or by filling in an evaluation sheet. It is this deliberate, planned evaluation which this book has concentrated upon, offering the reader a range of 'tools' to assist this process. Thus we can measure and judge how effective the learning experience has been in ensuring that desired goals are achieved. These planned processes can be carried out by an individual or by a group. They may involve introspection (self-appraisal), seeking students' and colleagues' opinions, measuring knowledge/skills acquired. Evaluation can also be used to attempt to judge the value or worth of the learning experience as a whole. This goes beyond measuring whether particular goals have been achieved, posing the question as to whether the goals are themselves worthwhile.

It is up to you, the reader, to decide what to evaluate, why and then how. In taking this decision, I have argued that *usefulness* should be the most important factor. No evaluation should be started if there is no prospect of its being useful to someone. I have argued, moreover, that *first and foremost it should be useful to students and teachers.* Then considerations of *feasibility* should begin. How feasible is it in terms of costs and time? There are hard questions to be asked and answered about cost-effectiveness. At this stage, do not be deterred by lack of resources. These can often be found if you can demonstrate the usefulness and feasibility of the evaluation.

Resources are currently being made available by some employers under the aegis of 'quality assurance'. But, in the main, when sums of money are calculated and allocated to monitoring, evaluation and review activities, they are pitifully inadequate. When educationalists are urged to follow the models of industry and commerce, to create a high quality 'product', to market it effectively and to become to a greater extent self-financing, we must, at the very least, ensure that we receive proper financing for 'quality assurance'. Those same industries we are urged to emulate spend at least 10% of their total costs on quality assurance. Which college puts 10% of its budget into evaluation activities? It is up to those of us who wish to properly evaluate our courses, who need the resources to do so, to put our case convincingly, to plan and implement effective systems of evaluation.

Many employers are not yet sure of how they wish to conduct their quality assurance procedures. *The time is ripe for students and teachers to come forward with their proposals.* As well as providing us with the resources we need, this can ensure that practitioners and consumers of educational services play their proper part in shaping, defining and controlling 'quality assurance'. We may thereby ensure that *useful* evaluation takes place.

Useful evaluation must be designed individually for different situations. There can be no single set of questions, no particular approach which can be used to evaluate (and thereby compare) all educational services. This is the mistake too often made by bureaucrats. *There is no one best way to conduct an evaluation. Every evaluation situation is unique.* Evaluators have to respond to each situation individually. But, at the same time, they must create systems which avoid unnecessary (and expensive) replication. Personal qualities and interpersonal skills are at least as important in an evaluator as the ability to design questionnaires, use information technology systems etc; more important, in fact, as methodology can be learned.

It is important to evaluate the evaluation. Have we made the right choices about what to evaluate? How representative is the steering committee which makes the major decisions? How do people involved feel about the evaluation? Have we chosen the most appropriate methods? Are they cost-effective? Do they yield useful information? Is the information acted upon? Do the changes which result lead to a better service? Do we as evaluators remain open, or do we develop and defend entrenched positions? Questions such as these must be asked and answered if we are to ensure that evaluation is effective and that it continues to respond to changing situations.

Finally, how can we equip ourselves to carry out evaluation? There is a need to read, to think and to discuss ideas with colleagues and students. Because most of the work that has been done on evaluation has been carried out in the U.S.A., much of the available literature comes from there. In America there is an Evaluation Research Society and an Evaluation Network with its own newsletter. A Joint Committee of Standards for Educational Evaluation has been meeting there for several years. **M. Q. Patton** (1981) offers a comprehensive insight into their workings and an excellent bibliography. The references and suggested readings below offer an opportunity to the interested would-be evaluator to begin reading.

Numerous appendices follow. There is no attempt here to offer blue-prints. How could there be, when each evaluation will differ from the next? What is offered is a set of models for different evaluation techniques which the reader can adapt.

It will be much easier and more enjoyable to carry out evaluation if it is done in collaboration with others. But if initially that proves difficult, every teacher can start in a modest way to evaluate her/his own course. *This is the final recommendation – start small, start soon.* I have no doubt that once a teacher starts to evaluate, the rewards are so great in comparison to the efforts made that the process will continue. *Evaluation can be a creative, enjoyable and energizing experience.*

References and Suggested Reading

Adelman, C. and Alexander, R. J. (1982) *The Self-Evaluating Institution,* Methuen. (A detailed account of the processes and impact of a major programme of evaluation in two colleges. Particularly interesting accounts of what happened as the evaluations were taking place.)

D.E.S./W.O. (1987) *Managing Colleges Efficiently,* (A report of a study of efficiency in non-advanced Further Education for the government and Local Authority Association. This report introduced six Efficiency Indicators which have formed the basis of much subsequent Quality Assurance and evaluation.)

Edwards, J. (1986) *Working Class Adult Education in Liverpool: A Radical Approach,* Manchester Monographs. (The book describes the *Second Chance to Learn* course based upon information yielded by more than five years of evaluation. It is an account of the course and of the impact of evaluation upon that course.)

Flood-Page, C. (1984) *Student Evaluation of Teaching: The American Experience,* Society for Research into Higher Education, London. (This book makes a strong case for student evaluation of teaching and explores the pros and cons. It offers a few interesting examples of rating scales and questionnaires. The book draws extensively on research conducted largely in the U.S.A.)

F.E.S.C. (1988) *Client Satisfaction: Monitoring Quality* . (A Coombe Lodge Special Report, Volume 20, Number 12. A Report of the Responsive College Programme, which explains the rationale behind the SPOC/EPOC system and provides many examples of questionnaires.)

F.E.U. (1989) *Towards an Educational Audit.* (In this document the FEU recommend ways of 'auditing' a college or other educational institution. Auditing here refers to measurement of the quality of services offered as perceived by students/ employers/the local community, as well as the measurement of efficiency, effectiveness of college services. The document gives an overview of institutional evaluation and indicates the direction which colleges etc. will be likely to take as a result of the Education Reform Act 1988.)

F.E.U. (1983) *College-Based Course Evaluation.* (A report of 'in-house' evaluation conducted by four colleges, including BEC National courses. Many valuable ideas and examples are included, plus an exploration of evaluation processes and problems.)

Gibbs, G., Habeshaw, S. and Habeshaw, T. (1988) *53 Interesting Ways to Appraise Your Teaching,* **Technical Educational Services Ltd.** (A collection of ideas for teachers to use, each presented simply and briefly. Many of the suggestions would need little or no adaptation, making it easy for any teacher to get started.)

Lacey, C. and Lawton, D. (1981) *Issues in Accountability and Evaluation,* **Methuen.** (A collection of papers presented at a national seminar by lecturers and professors who explore areas of concern about the use of evaluation in curriculum development. Although it refers to schools, the issues raised need to be considered by anyone involved in evaluation in adult and further education.)

Mace, J. and Yarnit, M. (eds) (1987) *Time Off to Learn,* **Methuen.** (Chapter 9, 'Second Chance to Learn, Liverpool', is based upon research carried out by *Second Chance* students and tutors into the experience of workers taking time out to study.)

Miller, J. and Dower, A. (1989) *Improving Quality in Further Education. A Guide for Teachers in Course Teams,* **Consultants at Work, Crown Copyright.**

Miller J. and Inniss, S. (1990) *The Strategic Management of a*

Quality Further Education Service. A Working Paper for LEA Officers and College Principals, Consultants at Work, Crown Copyright.

Miller, J. and Inniss, S. (1990) *Managing Quality Improvement in Further Education. A Guide for Middle Managers,* Consultants at Work, Crown Copyright.

Parlett, M. and Hamilton, D. (1972) *Evaluation as Illumination: A New Approach to the Study of Innovative Programs.* Occasional Papers No. 9, Centre for Research in the Educational Sciences, University of Edinburgh, Reprinted in Hamilton, D. et al (1977) *Beyond the Numbers Game: A Reader in Educational Evaluation,* MacMillan, London.

Patton, M. Q. (1978) *Utilization-Focused Evaluation,* Sage Publications. (As the title suggests, the emphasis here is upon the utility of evaluation. It contains valuable guides – the 'do's and don'ts' – illustrated by practical examples and would help anyone designing evaluation/research.)

Patton, M. Q. (1980) *Qualitative Evaluation Methods,* Sage Publications. (Practical advice and examples derived from many years of experience as an evaluator in the U.S.A.)

Patton, M. Q. (1981) *Creative Evaluation,* Sage Publications. (A stimulating, readable account of evaluation techniques emphasising throughout a creative and eclectic approach.)

Rowntree, D. (1982) *Educational Technology in Curriculum Development,* (2nd Edition) Harper and Row. (Chapter 6 'Evaluation and Improvement', provides an excellent introduction to the concept and practice of evaluation.)

Rowntree, D. (1987) *Assessing Students: How Shall We Know Them?* Kogan Page. (A comprehensive guide to assessment of students' learning which discusses the uses and limitations of different assessment methods.)

Ruddock, R. (1981) *Evaluation: A Consideration of Principles and Methods,* Manchester Monographs.

Stufflebeam, D. (1980) 'An Interview with D. L. Stufflebeam'. *Educational Evaluation and Policy Analysis,* 1980, 2, 90.

Tyler, R. W., Gagne, R. and Scriven, M. (1967) *Perspectives of Curriculum Evaluation,* Rand McNally, Chicago.

U.D.A.C.E. (1989) *Performance Indicators and the Education of Adults,* **N.I.A.C.E.** and

U.D.A.C.E. (1989) *Understanding Learning Outcomes,* **N.I.A.C.E.** (These two Development Papers examine some of the difficulties of evaluating adult education, particularly in the 'Community Education' sector. Models for institutional evaluation are proposed which place learning outcomes at the heart of the evaluation process.)

Yarnit, M. (1980) 'Second chance to Learn – Liverpool: Class and Adult Education' in **Thompson, J. L. (ed)** *Adult Education for a Change,* **Hutchinson.** (This chapter describes the *Second Chance to Learn* course.)

Hall, Budd. Look out for his numerous papers on Participatory Research in a variety of educational journals.

Addresses

Consultants at Work
P.O. Box 19, High Street
Ware
Hertfordshire
SG12 0LE

F.E.S.C. (Further Education Staff College)
The Librarian
The Further Education Staff College
Coombe Lodge
Blagdon
Bristol
BS18 6RG
(Information Bank Working Papers on staff-appraisal and self-evaluation.)

F.E.U. (Further Education Unit)
FEU Information Centre
Grove House
2 Orange St
London
WC2H 7WA

U.D.A.C.E.
Christopher House,
94B London Road
Leiceister LE2 0QS

Judith Edwards
c/o **W.E.A.**
7/8 Bluecoat Chambers
School Lane
Liverpool
L1 3BX

Elizabeth Whale (Adviser for Monitoring and Evaluation)
City of Birmingham Education Department
Margaret Street
Birmingham
B3 3BU

(Birmingham's Quality Development Team intends to produce a practical handbook on monitoring and evaluation for managers and practitioners.)

List of Appendices

N.B. In order to save space in the following pages, the blank spaces usually left for replies to open questions have been omitted. In creating similar questionnaires, you should leave an appropriate space to guide students about the amount of detail you would wish them to supply.

APPENDIX 1A
Self-Evaluation I

From F.E.S.C. paper 2304 "Staff Appraisal –
the Model of Self-Evaluation" by D. Marsh, 1987
(F.E.S.C. papers available from the address on page 97)

Work Review

Which aspects of your work have given you the most/least satisfaction?

(a) Most

(b) Least

In which spheres of work activity do you feel your particular strengths/weaknesses lie?

(a) Strengths

(b) Weaknesses

What problems or difficulties affecting your job performance have you encountered and how could they have been overcome?

Future Development

Do you consider that there is any action that could be taken to help improve your performance?

In which areas of work would you prefer to develop?

Do you have specific action in mind which would help in this development?

Other points on which you would like to comment.

APPENDIX 1B
Self-Evaluation II

From F.E.S.C. paper 2304 "Staff Appraisal – the Model of Self-Evaluation" by D. Marsh, 1987
(F.E.S.C. papers available from the address on page 97)

The Process of Self-Evaluation

To evaluate individual performance and corporate effectiveness, questions under the following main headings should be generated.

1. Responsibility and Accountability
   (a) For whom, and for what, precisely do I have responsibility?
   (b) To whom am I directly accountable for those?
   (c) How is that accountability ensured?

2. Authority
   (a) What precisely may I do on my own authority?
   (b) For what do I have to seek the authority of others?
   (c) Who has that authority?

3. Duties
   (a) What are my regular duties? (i.e. those routine duties for which I am responsible.)
   (b) What duties must show key results? (i.e. priorities)
   (c) What are those key results?

4. Tasks
   What are the tasks I have to accomplish? (i.e. those parts of my job beyond routine duties.)

5. Performance Criteria
   (a) By what criteria is my performance in the job measured?
   (b) Are those criteria agreed and specified?
   (c) How do I judge the performance of people for whom I have responsibility and authority?

6. Objectives
   (a) What are the objectives of my job? Which are the key objectives?
   (b) Are they specified?
   (c) Are they agreed with myself and with others?

7. Targets
   (a) Are objectives specified in terms of targets, ie. attainable, measurable targets for the job?
   (b) What difficulties make target attainment difficult for me?
   (c) What support systems do I have/need?

8. Performance Measures
   How is present and future performance measured?

9. Development
   (a) What can be identified as present/future needs for development in order to meet duties, tasks, objectives and targets?
   (b) What is my job improvement plan?

APPENDIX 2
Tutor Self-Evaluation

This relates particularly to the responsibilities of a teacher in her/his teaching environment. **From F.E.S.C. paper 2304 "Staff Appraisal – the Model of Self-Evaluation" by D. Marsh, 1987** (F.E.S.C. papers available from the address on page 97)

Consider your effectiveness under each of these headings, then set yourself specific targets for improvement.

Organisation of subject matter
- self-preparation
- knowledge of material and updating of knowledge
- long-term planning: syllabus design, sequence of teaching units, choice of appropriate materials and methods
- short-term planning (single units): lesson, lecture, tutorial, seminar, workshop, assignment, project.

Management of learning
- class management
- presentation, development and consolidation of work
- motivation of students and maintenance of interest
- attention to individuals
- assessment and monitoring
- setting and correction of assignments
- use of teaching aids and materials
- liaison with other course tutors and colleagues
- contribution to curriculum development
- contribution to work of college as a whole
- attendance at relevant courses, conferences and seminars
- liaison with industry

Personal qualities
- attendance, punctuality and timekeeping
- voice and diction: audibility and clarity
- appropriateness of language to situation
- rapport with students and manner in class, counselling and interviewing
- involvement of students in class management
- sensitivity to others
- attention to administrative requirements
- capacity for professional self-evaluation and evaluation of students

---

APPENDIX 3
Evaluation of Teaching (by colleagues and/or students)

From F.E.S.C. paper 1638 'Appraisal Systems' by C. Turner, 1981
(F.E.S.C. papers available from the address on page 97)

Course: _____

Date: _____

Lecturer: _____

	Essentially true for me	Usually true for me	Rarely true for me	Not true for me
1. Presents the material clearly and logically				
2. Enables the student to understand the basic principles of the subject				
3. Can be clearly heard				
4. Makes the material intelligibly meaningful				
5. Adequately covers the ground in the course				
6. Maintains continuity in the course				
7. Is constructive and helpful in giving criticism				
8. Shows an expert knowledge of the subject				
9. Includes in the lectures material which is not readily accessible in textbooks				
10. Adopts an appropriate pace when teaching				
11. Is concise				
12. Illustrates the practical applications of the theory of the subject				
13. Avoids trivial time-filling material in classes				
14. Stimulates students to think independently				
15. Does not ridicule wrong answers				
16. Helpfully spaces requirements of written work				
17. Imparts enthusiasm for the subject				
18. Refers to the latest developments in the subject				
19. Sets clear objectives for the students				
20. Readily considers students' viewpoints				
21. Has a good sense of humour				

	Essentially true for me	Usually true for me	Rarely true for me	Not true for me
22. Writes legibly on the chalkboard				
23. Appears confident and at ease when teaching				
24. Allows questions during lectures				
25. Motivates students to work willingly				
26. Points out the links between the subject and related subjects				
27. Is well-informed in fields related to the subject				
28. Avoids an excess of factual details				
29. Provides full references to books, articles etc.				
30. Organises chalkboard work clearly				
31. Has a sympathetic attitude towards students				
32. Avoids forcing her/his own point of view				
33. Is spontaneously friendly				
34. Appreciates students' own accomplishments				
35. Appears to enjoy teaching				
36. Uses appropriate illustrative teaching aids (slides, films, programmes, models, charts etc.)				
37. Has a pleasantly modulated voice				
38. Tries to relate the course to broad human values and goals				
39. Has a good vocabulary				
40. Avoids distracting personal mannerisms				
41. Has a democratic approach				
42. Is skilful in drawing chalkboard diagrams				

Please add any further comments

APPENDIX 4
Evaluation Targeting and Planning Workpack

Printed by kind permission of **Elizabeth Whale,** (Formerly co-ordinator of the Birmingham Quality Development Unit. Address on page 98)

These worksheets can be used by individuals or groups to help them to decide which aspects of a service they should evaluate and to plan their activities.

Before a group meets to decide upon their evaluation activities, members can be asked to complete worksheets 1 and 2 individually. This allows the group to progress much more rapidly in taking decisions. Worksheet 3 is completed as a joint exercise after discussion of each group member's individual worksheets.

Worksheets 4, 5 and 6 are then completed separately for each evaluative question. Multiple copies of these are required so that a set can be prepared for each aspect of evaluation to be undertaken. Individual group members can be asked to complete sheets 4, 5 and 6 and bring these back to the group for discussion/agreement. This speeds up the planning processes.

In some groups an individual or small working group can each be allocated one or more evaluative questions and given the responsibility for carrying out the evaluation. Worksheets 4, 5 and 6 will help them plan their activities.

WORKSHEET 1
WHAT DO YOU WANT TO EVALUATE?
Write down all the areas of interest, problems/concerns (however big or small) you would like to investigate further. Write each one down in the form of a question e.g.

1. How successful have our (Access) students been in obtaining qualifications in higher education?
2. Do our guidance procedures ensure that we accept the right students onto our courses?
3.
4.
5.
6.
7.
8. etc.

WORKSHEET 2

WHERE ARE YOU GOING TO START?

Referring to your questions on Worksheet I, list in order of priority the areas you want to focus on.

Write down each area in the form of a question.

EVALUATIVE QUESTION	INFORMATION REQUIRED	SOURCE OF INFORMATION

WORKSHEET 3
WHERE ARE YOU GOING TO START?

Think again about your priorities for evaluation in the light of:

(i)   discussion with colleagues

(ii)   what is practical in your working situation.

Reprioritise if necessary.

EVALUATIVE QUESTION	INFORMATION REQUIRED	SOURCE OF INFORMATION

WORKSHEET 4

GETTING THE INFORMATION YOU NEED

You need to use a separate copy of Worksheet 4 for each evaluative question.

Evaluative question	
Methods of gathering information	
Who will be involved?	
How long will it take?	
When will it happen?	
What resources do you need?	

WORKSHEET 5

PROVIDING INFORMATION

You need to use a separate copy of Worksheet 5 for each evaluative question.

Who is interested/should be interested in the evaluation information?
Why are they/should they be interested?   **What will they want to know about?**
How shall we give them the information, in what format?   **When shall we provide it?**

WORKSHEET 6

TASK LIST

You need to use a separate copy of Worksheet 6 for each evaluative question.

You now need to plan exactly how you are going to get your evaluation project off the ground. It might help if you write yourself a list of tasks in the order in which you have to do them, with approximate dates.

Task	Start Date	Finish Date
1.		
2.		
3.		
4.		
5.		
6.		
7.		
8.		
9.		
10.		
11.		
12.		
13.		
14.		
15.		
16.		
17.		
18.		
etc.		

APPENDIX 5
End of Term Review

This is a sample of a review carried out on the *Second Chance to Learn* course, Liverpool. It took place at the end of the first term of the year-long, part-time course. There were approximately 25 students present (all adults) and the whole process (small group discussions and plenary session) lasted two and a half hours. Written instructions were distributed and discussed before students divided into groups. The final paragraph of these instructions was discussed fully in order to encourage students to give honest replies.

Instructions for carrying out the review.

Please divide into four equal groups (approximately five or six per group). Choose a chairperson, who will ensure that:
  (a) all group members have the opportunity to comment upon each question, if they wish;
  (b) time is allocated to ensure that all questions can be properly considered.
Choose a reporter who will:
  (a) note briefly the replies given to each question;
  (b) report these back (verbally) to the full group of all students and tutors at the end of the morning.
N.B. Please make sure that minority comments are reported as well as ones which are widely agreed upon.

Each group should comment upon the *General Questions*. In addition, Group 1 will please answer the questions on Tutorials; Group 2 on History Workshops; Group 3 on Study Skills and Group 4 on Writers' Workshops. Divide your time equally between General Questions and your group's Special Questions.

We suggest you allow 5 minutes for silent reading and thinking about the General Questions, before students begin to make comments. Repeat this process when you move on to your Special Questions. If time permits, you might like to allow about 10 to 15 minutes for pairs of students to talk about their responses to the General Questions, before commenting to the group. This can be repeated with the answers to the Special Questions.

When you answer the questions, please answer honestly and give concrete examples wherever you can. Tutors welcome honest feedback, both praise and criticism. We want to improve the course and our teaching, and can only do this with your help. You would not want us to pretend and give false comments when we help you to improve your work. You want to know what is right, what is wrong and how to put it right. We want the same from you. Please help us.

General Questions

1. Have you enjoyed this term? Why/Why not?
2. In what ways has the course come up to your expectations?
3. What skills have you developed i.e. what things can you now do better than you could before?
4. List any 'niggles' you have about the course generally.
5. Have you found it boring – moving too slowly? or too hard? going too fast? or is it about right for you personally?
6. Are you expected to do too much homework and preparation? or is there too little, or is it about right?
7. What have you enjoyed most about your first term?
8. What have you most disliked?
9. What have you found hardest to do?
10. What changes or additions would you like to suggest for next term?
11. Do you have any anxieties about the next 2 terms?
12. Some students have left the course. Do you have any idea why?
13. Do you have any questions you'd like to ask us?

Special Questions (these have been written by the tutor(s) responsible for each part of the course)

Group 1 – Tutorials

1. How many tutorials have you had this term and how long did each one last?
2. Do you have your tutorial on the same day as you attend the course, or do you return another day?
3. Will each person individually please write down a few notes about what you do in a typical tutorial then compare your answers. Please discuss in detail what you find are the most useful ways of spending tutorial time.
4. What could your tutor do to help you more?
5. If you are to attend tutorials next term once every 2 weeks, what activities could you usefully do in the week between? Would it be a good idea to come in and work with other students?

Group 2 – History Workshops

This term you have covered the following topics in the afternoon workshops:

History Workshop

1. Growth of Port/Development of Wealthy Class
2. Liverpool's Working Class
3. Liverpool and the Slave Trade
4. Liverpool's Black Community
5. The Irish in Liverpool

etc.

Please talk about each of these sessions and try to answer the following questions about each:

(a) How useful did you find it?
(b) How enjoyable did you find it?
(c) How could the session have been changed to make it more beneficial for you and/or for the group as a whole?

General

Discussion has been used a lot in the workshops, sometimes in small groups and sometimes with all the students together.

1. What are the benefits of this way of learning?
2. What are the problems?
3. Can you think of any solutions?
4. How well are all members of the group learning to chair the small groups and give report backs?

Workshop Notes

1. Do you usually/always/rarely, study these carefully before the workshop?
2. Are they lengthy/difficult/easy/boring/just right?
3. Do you usually write answers to any questions in the notes?
4. Have you read any of the recommended books yet? If not, why not?

Next Term

1. Would you like to suggest any changes in the workshop notes or the workshops themselves for next term?
2. Can you think of any topics you would particularly like us to cover?

Group 3 – Study Skills

There have been 7 study skills sessions this term:

1. Introduction – Solving Study Problems
2. The visit to the Central Library
3. Learning from Group Discussion – Skills of Chairing and Reporting back
4. Notetaking I – from books/papers
5. Notetaking II – from radio broadcast
6. Notetaking III – from 'Question Time' (TV)
7. Reading Textbooks

Please talk about each of these sessions and try to answer the following questions about each:

(a) How useful did you find it?
(b) How enjoyable did you find it?
(c) How could the session be changed to make it more beneficial?
(d) How confident do you now feel about doing the skill in question and about your capacity to improve it over the coming months?

Generally

1. Have we chosen the most important skills to cover first or would you prefer to have had workshops on other study skills topics (e.g. essay writing) this term and left some of this term's topics until later? If so, what changes would you have liked?
2. Do you find time to practice at home or elsewhere?
3. Do you *regularly* discuss study skills work with your tutor?
4. Do you show your work to your fellow students and make real efforts to learn from one another?
5. Are there areas of study skills work which are not covered on the course which you feel should be?

Group 4 – Writers' Workshops

1. Did you enjoy them? Why/Why not?
    Could anything be altered so that you enjoy them more?
2. Did they benefit you in any way? If so, how?
    If not, could anything be altered so that you would benefit more?
3. What comments can you make on the way the course was taught that would be helpful for the future?
4. Do you think that students should be given specific tasks in writing?
    e.g. Write something about yourself
    A day out
    A job that I liked
5. Would you have liked a workshop where time was set aside to write?
6. Would you like to have had more time spent on grammar, spelling, punctuation?
7. Did you try writing something you had never tried before?
8. Did the workshop improve your confidence? Did it lessen your embarrassment in reading your work out in public?
9. Would you have liked to have spent more time analysing the works of great writers (the 'classics') bearing in mind that this would have meant less time for your own writing?
10. Has the workshop changed your attitude to poetry? If so, how?
12. Knowing what you now know, what sort of writers' workshop would best serve a similar group of students on future courses?

APPENDIX 6
Examples of Useful Questions for Regular Evaluation

These are just a few examples of the sorts of questions you could ask. Some of them wouldn't be relevant. You will be able to think of a lot more which would be more relevant to your courses.

It is important to remember to get the atmosphere right – to help everyone (tutors and students) see that this isn't a threatening exercise but, rather, a way of making the teaching/learning more enjoyable and effective for everyone concerned.

It is also important not to try to ask too many questions at once. It is better to choose a few really important areas and to encourage students to think about the answers and ask them *why* they answered in a particular way. You will get far more out of that than by asking lots of questions and getting a lot of quick yes/no answers.

The answers need recording – either by using a cassette recorder or by having someone take notes during the evaluation. Ask students' permission to record their answers.

These are the kind of questions which need to be asked *regularly* during a course. *Don't wait until the whole course ends before you ask them.* You may prefer to spend a few minutes at the end of every session asking some of these questions, or you may prefer to set a longer period of time aside for evaluation every few weeks.

1. What do you now know or understand that you didn't before?
2. What can you do now that you couldn't do before? *(e.g. write an essay, address the group, put your point of view more confidently, converse in another language, etc.)*
3. What skills do you still need to develop which you can reasonably expect to on this course?
4. In what ways do you feel different now from how you felt before you began the course?
5. What do you still want to know about?
6. Think back to what you hoped to get out of this course.
    (a) Are you getting out of it what you hoped to?
    (b) What aren't you getting out of it that you hoped to?

116

(c) Are you getting any other things out of it that you hadn't expected to?

7. (a) What have you enjoyed most so far, and why?
   (b) What have you disliked most so far, and why?

8. Do you have any comments to make which would help us plan and/or teach the course better?

9. Generally speaking do you find the course moves
   (a) too quickly for you to be able to understand?
   (b) too slowly – so you are bored?
   (c) is the pace just about right?

10. Do you feel that the students are encouraged to join in and give their opinions
    (a) not often enough?
    (b) too often?
    (c) about right?

11. Can you get hold of the books the tutor recommends you to read?
    If not, does that affect what you get out of the course? Can you suggest any ways to solve this problem?

12. Do you find it easy to speak up to give your opinions during the course? If not, could anything be done to make this easier?

13. Have your opinions on the subject(s) you are studying changed in any way? If so, how?

14. How do you think the tutor or group could deal with the following problems?
    (List any problems there are e.g. People coming late. Some people talking too much, dominating the session etc.)

15. Would you prefer
    (a) to look briefly at a different topic each week to get an overview of the subject?
    (b) to examine fewer topics in greater depth – each lasting several sessions perhaps?

16. Do you prefer to spend more time
    (a) listening to the lecturer?
    (b) joining in group discussions?
    (c) doing practical tasks?
    Why?

17. Ask the students to look back over each individual session in

117

turn and consider the following questions:

(a) did you understand that session?

(b) was it enjoyable?

(c) did the tutor try to put (i) too much into it, or (ii) too little, or (iii) was it about right?

(d) were the materials (books/films etc.) used suitable? Did they help you understand it better or not?

18. (a) Do you feel that your group gets on well together?

(b) Do you experience any problems with group relationships?

(c) Can you think of ways to help people get to know each other better?

Now try thinking of some more questions of your own to add to this list.

APPENDIX 7
Guidelines for Writing a Questionnaire
(Issued to students on Second Chance To Learn)

Here are some suggestions you might like to think about if you are planning to use a questionnaire as part of an enquiry, survey or piece of research. These ideas may guide you and help you avoid some pitfalls. Because it is very hard to anticipate all the pitfalls, it is a good idea to try a pilot questionnaire. Try asking a small sample of people to answer your questionnaire and then ask them if they found any questions confusing or difficult. Check their answers and see if you can make sense of them. It is surprising how many problems quickly come to light and can be put right before you send out your questionnaire. It is useful to analyse this sample of questionnaires because you may uncover problems and so re-write questions.

Thinking up Questions
Following these steps may help you think up questions and avoid irrelevant ones.

1. First of all think carefully and talk to others about:

(a) what you want to find out

(b) why you want to know it

(c) what use you intend to make of the information, and write down the answers to these questions. This will help you begin to think clearly about the purpose of your research and it helps inspiration to flow.

2. Brainstorm – i.e. think up any questions at all and write down. No censorship. At this stage don't try to decide whether they are relevant or useful. Anything goes when you are brainstorming. It is good to do this in a group as you will spark off ideas in one another. Write all down.

3. Go through each of your questions carefully now and see if each provides answers to the points you wrote down in 1a, b and c. Do you have questions to find out all you wanted to know? If not, now is the time to think up some additional questions to cover any areas you have left out.

4. Now organise your questions in a rough way, grouping similar ones together and deciding the best order. Don't worry at this

stage about getting the wording or layout right. That comes later.
5. Show your list to anyone else who you think might be able to make helpful comments or suggest new questions.

Writing your Questions

Now you have your list of questions, you will have to decide how best to lay them out. Your choice will depend on how you are going to use your questionnaire. First decide whether you will:

(a) take this questionnaire with you and use it when you interview someone, or

(b) post or give it to people and ask them to post the reply to you (with no opportunity to discuss the questions).

Writing Questions for Conducting Interviews

If you are using your questionnaire as a tool for interviews, it is easier than drafting a postal questionnaire. If you have not managed to write a question down clearly, you can explain it to your interviewee in whatever way you need to. So, getting the words exactly right is not quite as vital. It still matters, though. You need to write/say your question in a way which does not lead your interviewee to a particular answer. If your question isn't clear, it means that you have not thought out exactly what you want to know.

Ask yourself:

(i) Are you going to spend a long time interviewing a number of individuals (half an hour or more, maybe using a cassette player to back up your notetaking)?

or (ii) do you want to carry out a large number of very quick interviews each lasting just a few minutes at most, in the way market researchers do when they stop people in the streets to ask questions?

For a lengthy interview, you should use more *open* questions.

For a quick interview, *closed* questions are better.

What is the difference?

Open Questions: useful for obtaining opinions

If you want someone's opinion you can ask them like this:
What do you think about the Writers' Workshop on Second Chance?
Honest opinions please. What are its strong points?
What could be improved?

120

Make sure you ask questions which are precise and people can answer.

e.g. How well prepared did the teacher seem to be in your opinion?
not *How good was the teacher?*

Note how much more specific the first question is. Avoid words like *good* as they are far too vague.

Closed Questions: **useful for obtaining factual information which can then be expressed as percentages.**

The same kind of information about someone's opinion of the writers' workshop could be gained by a series of short questions like this:

	Usually	Sometimes	Rarely
1. Did you think the writers' workshop was enjoyable?	☐	☐	☐
2. Did the writers' workshop inspire you to write at home?	☐	☐	☐
3. Do you think the writers' workshop was ....? etc.	☐	☐	☐

Then they tick the boxes as appropriate.

The Pros and Cons of *Open* and *Closed* Questions

Open questions leave the field wide open. There is little risk of directing or channelling interviewees to think in particular ways. There is less chance of you missing out something important from your own list of closed questions. With gentle inquisitive prompting you can get your interviewee to keep adding to the opinion. You don't have to accept the first answer. You can then say, *'Do you have any other thoughts about the writers' workshop?'* and if there is no reply you can be a bit more direct with your prompt e.g. *'Did you ever find it boring?'* etc.

Closed questions are particularly useful if you are seeking factual information (who, where, when, how many) or if you don't have much time to let the interviewee think about her/his answers (e.g. in the street). They direct attention to particular key points rapidly. Their main limitation is obvious – people might have come up with very different answers but, because you have not asked, they can only answer what you have asked.

The other limitation of Yes/No, or even Yes/No/Don't Know, is that it is just too rigid a way to answer lots of questions.

e.g. *Did you enjoy the writers workshop?* YES   NO

Lots of people would think – *'Well sometimes I did, but sometimes I was bored and a few times I hated it.'* Those boxes don't give much scope for complex human reactions.

Nevertheless they are useful, especially in quick interviews (and even more so in postal questionnaires). By asking particular questions you can guarantee an answer to each. In open questions, interviewees may just not think to reply about enjoyment or boredom or whatever it is you'd like to know about.

The other advantage of closed questions comes if you conduct hundreds of interviews. With such large numbers, analysing open questions is a real headache. Counting up 'yeses' and 'noes' is far easier. So, though they are harder to think up and write, they are easier to analyse.

Broadly speaking then *the size of your sample* will help you decide whether to use open or closed questions:

small sample/lengthy interviews – more open questions
large sample/street interviews/postal questionnaires – more closed questions.

Prompting

Below are samples of *prompt* questions devised by *Second Chance* students as they prepared themselves to carry out individual interviews. First ask the questions without prompting and note the reply. Then use the prompts, one by one, to draw out more and more information. Prompts cannot be fully prepared in advance, but lists such as these can prove helpful.

1. Have you gone on to any courses or gone on learning in any other way since Second Chance to Learn?

> **Prompts** – **what were they – list all**
> **– why did you choose those particular ones?**

2. Did Second Chance influence your decision in any way at all?

> **Prompts** – **subject interests**
> **– new horizons opened up**
> **– confidence**

3. Please compare your experience of any courses you have since attended with your experience of Second Chance.

> **Prompts** – **formality**
> **– helpfulness**
> **– enjoyment**
> **– problems encountered on courses**
> **– co-operation and competition**
> **– personal help from tutors**

Writing Questions for Postal Questionnaires
(The guidance offered in this section is applicable to the designing of any questionnaire, whether it is distributed by post or not)

There are many advantages in using postal questionnaires – mainly to do with sample size. Only postage costs will limit the size of your sample. You can hope for a much larger sample than if you conduct interviews, which are very time-consuming. However, there are a number of potential problems which you have to overcome. These are dealt with below under a) general points and b) writing questions.

a) General Points
i) You must write a cover letter to fully explain who you are and why you are asking these questions. People are, quite rightly, very suspicious and if you don't succeed in overcoming their suspicions, they will not reply.

ii) Wherever possible make sure the replies will be anonymous – and tell people in the letter that's how it will be. You cannot always offer this, however, so don't deceive people.

iii) Enclose a stamped, self-addressed envelope (costly, but essential) and either leave space for replies on the questionnaire and/or enclose paper.

iv) Give a date to return by – usually a couple of weeks is about right. Any longer and people put it away till later and then forget.

v) Do not make it too long or complicated. This is the hardest of all. The temptation to ask too much is dreadfully hard to resist, but you will lose out in the end. The longer it is, the fewer replies you are likely to get. Complicated questions lead to such a muddle that you cannot make sense of the answers.

vi) After your deadline has passed, if you can afford postage, write again to remind people to reply. It is amazing how many just forget. Some could have lost the whole thing. Can you afford to send another copy and another stamped addressed envelope? Your persistence will probably pay off if you can manage it.

b) Writing Questions for Postal Questionnaires

Once again you are faced with the dilemma of choosing open and closed questions. This time it is very important to remember there is no chance to explain – so questions have to be clear, simply worded and not 'leading' or directing the respondent to any particular reply. Here are a few ideas to help you.

Open Questions

As before, you simply ask a number of wide open questions.

What do you think about the writers' workshop? Honest opinions please. What were its strong points? What could be improved?

Then you leave as much space as you hope they will fill.

Closed Questions

You can make a series of short statements and see if they agree or disagree with them. First you must write:

Please tick the appropriate box like this.

Please do not use any other way of marking your answer,

if that is what you want people to do. It may seem unnecessary and obvious, but it is surprising how many different ways people have of indicating their answers and some change midway through their answers and it becomes impossible to work out what they wish to indicate. Try to ensure that you don't muddle your respondents by altering the way you want them to mark the questionnaire. If you are consistent, there is less chance of them getting confused.

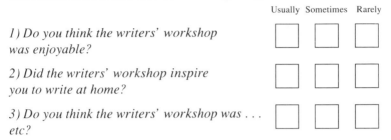

Usually Sometimes Rarely

1) Do you think the writers' workshop was enjoyable?

2) Did the writers' workshop inspire you to write at home?

3) Do you think the writers' workshop was . . . etc?

Then you have to produce a list containing all the possible answers you can anticipate, or that you want to know more about. You can end with an open question like:

> *Would you like to make any further comments about the writers' workshop?*

and leave a space.

The Pros and Cons of Open and Closed Questions

When you are using postal questionnaires, open questions may not be so valuable because very often people write down their first idea and it may not really reflect their fully considered opinion at all. Even if you leave a space of 4 or 5 lines, most people will only put one sentence like, *'It was okay most of the time'*. You can obtain a lot more information from a series of closed questions, provided they are worded clearly.

There is the additional advantage when later analysing your answers. Open questions produce such a very varied set of responses they are hard to analyse. On the other hand, closed questions do omit the possibility of that very variety of response just mentioned. You really have to weigh up the pros and cons yourself, or best of all, go for a mixed questionnaire with open and closed questions.

Common Pitfalls

1. Overlapping Categories

You may well need to collect information about age, gender, occupation, etc. because you may want to see if these factors make any difference to people's answers. First, only ask for this information if you think it is relevant – because it increases people's suspicion. Age may matter, but quite a lot of people feel defensive if you ask. So think carefully about your need of it.

e.g. Age. You may ask:

Please tick 20-30/30-40/40-50/50-60

That's wrong. What if a person is exactly 30 or 40 or 50? Which box would they tick?

Instead write: 20-29/30-39/40-49/50-59

If there are any categories like this in any of your questions, make sure they don't overlap. People should not feel confused about which to tick.

2. Leading Questions

Do you agree that writers' workshops were very enjoyable?

Putting questions like this does push for a particular answer. You have to try not to give away how you would like people to reply. This can be hard to avoid.

When you have done your first research survey and used question- naires, you will be able to add to the pitfalls list. Like everything else, you soon get better.

Analysing Questionnaires

There are numerous ways of carrying out an analysis of the data. The approach outlined below may help to get you started, but it is important for you to find the most suitable way yourself. This will depend upon how much data you have, your time available, whether you are analysing it alone or with others, who the report will be for.

1. Begin with the closed questions.

For each, make a grid of possible responses, then sift through the questionnaires ticking the appropriate column. You can either go through every questionnaire ticking the answer to question 1, then through again for question 2; or you can take one questionnaire at a time and tick the grids for every closed question.

This exercise is best performed in pairs, with one calling while the other ticks. You are less likely to lose your place (and have to start all over again).

NB Don't forget to have columns on your grid for 'no reply'

Q1

Usually	Sometimes	Rarely	No Reply

Transfer your final totals to a blank questionnaire sheet and convert raw totals to percentages with a calculator or using the formula.

$$\frac{\text{actual total}}{\text{possible total of replies}} \times 100$$

2. Open Questions

Before you begin to write anything, it is vital to get *an overview of the questionnaire as a whole and then of each particular open question.* Although this delays your analysis, it saves much time and effort and leads to greater clarity.

a. First take a random sample and rapidly read through responses to all the questions.

b. Then analyse questions one by one. Rapidly skim all (or as many as you reasonably can) of the replies to question 1. Stop and think. Are there any patterns in the replies: similar responses being made frequently? There almost always are. At this stage it is usually reasonably easy to think up some *general headings under which you can make notes of the replies.* Use a fresh sheet of paper for each heading preferably using one side only, so that all can be laid out – a very large desk top is ideal.

c. Go back through each questionnaire now and note the key point of each response under the various headings – each respondent may make several very different responses and each must be noted (not quoted verbatim) on the separate sheets. If two or more students make virtually identical points, place a tick for each time the comment is made. This will save you writing the same thing out several times, but will ensure that you know how frequently a particular response was made. That information is essential.

d. Whilst you are going through each questionnaire, you can at this stage identify quotations which you may want to use to enliven your report. You can copy these out or, to save time, you can simply use a highlighter pen on the questionnaire.

c. When the analysis of one question is completed, it is best to write up your commentary (in rough draft form) *before moving on to the next question*. If you analyse a dozen or more open questions and then begin the write-up, it is easy to get confused.

If a group of you are analysing a questionnaire, you can allocate one or more questions to each person in the group. That is much easier than giving each group member a pile of questionnaires to work on. If you decide to do this, it can influence your original questionnaire design. You may want groups of questions on separate pages, so that they can be divided up and allocated to different analysers.

After analysing all open questions and after writing drafts of commentary for each, pause before writing your final analysis. Decide who will read it and therefore how you wish to word it and lay it out. You may not wish to go through each question in the order it appears on the questionnaire. You could decide to use tables, diagrams, illustrations. Take all these decisions then write the final analysis, incorporating quotations if you can.

APPENDIX 8
Sample Questionnaire

Study Skills Course
End of Term Questionnaire

*I should be very grateful if you would complete this questionnaire straight away and return it to me within a week. I do not want you to sign it or indicate your identity in any way because I want you to feel free to make **honest** comments including criticisms. I really do want to know about any shortcomings and weaknesses in the course. It is the only way I can hope to improve it. Thank you for your help. Your ideas and comments will be used in future courses.*

1. What did you hope the Study Skills sessions would help you to do? (list anything you think of below)

   a)

   b)

   c)

   d)

   e)

   etc)

   Now place a tick by any items you have listed which you feel have been improved or achieved through Study Skills sessions and a cross by any which have not.

2. To help me evaluate each separate session, I'd like you to fill in the table over the page by ticking the columns to indicate whether you attended the session, whether you read the relevant section of **Learning Together** before the session and then, in the final column, I'd like you to give the session a score out of ten for usefulness:

   9-10 = very useful – couldn't really be improved on
   7-8 = good session but could be improved
   5-6 = reasonably useful
   3-4 = not very useful
   1-2 = waste of time or, even worse, left me feeling confused or anxious.

SESSION	Attended the Workshop	Read relevant material	Score out of 10
1. Introduction/solving study skills problems			
2. Library visit			
3. Using discussion as a way of learning; chairing and reporting			
4. Note-taking from books and papers			
5. Note-taking from speakers/T.V., etc.			
6. How to conduct research (three sessions)			
7. Reading a textbook			
8. Planning an essay			
9. Graphs			
10. Making the group work well			
11. Statistics			
12. Straight and crooked thinking (two sessions)			
13. Planning and presenting speeches (two sessions)			

3. Now please look back at any session you have scored anywhere between 1 and 6 and explain why each was unsatisfactory and any way you think each could be improved.

4. As a result of Study Skills workshops do you now find it easier to put the skills into practice?

a) usually

b) sometimes

c) occasionally   Please tick

d) never

5a. As a result of the Study Skills workshops do you now feel more confident than you did before the course about being able to go on to another course of study?

Yes ☐   No ☐   Please tick

5b. If you said 'No', please say what else you think could be done to help you.

6. As a result of the workshops do you now find you use some of the skills (such as chairing, note-taking, making a speech, etc.) in other areas of your life off the course?

Yes ☐   No ☐   Please tick

If 'Yes', please give examples.

7. Please comment on whether or not you have regularly used the book **Learning Together** and whether or not it has helped/confused etc.

8. If the Study Skills course has helped you (or your family) in any other ways which you have not already mentioned, please add any comments here.

9. Please comment on any weaknesses of the course generally, or of individual sessions, or of the style in which it was taught. Try to be honest.

10. Can you suggest any changes which would help me improve future Study Skills sessions?

APPENDIX 9
Sample of Interview Questions, with Additional 'Prompt' Questions in Boxes

(taken from a set of questions prepared by a group of *Second Chance to Learn* students before they carried out interviews to determine the effect the course had had upon former students)

LIFESTYLE

1. Did you feel satisfied with your lifestyle before coming on *2nd Chance*?

2. If not, did you hope *2nd Chance* would change it in some way? If so, in what ways?

3. Has your lifestyle changed in any ways since *2nd Chance*?

> Prompts – leisure
>   – family
>   – political
>   – community
>   – friends
>   – workplace
>   – reading habits
>   – going on courses
> (ask what they now do that's different from what they spent their time doing before *2nd Chance*)

4. Did *2nd Chance* play any part in changing your lifestyle? If so, please explain.

ATTITUDES
1. Have your attitudes to life changed in any ways since *2nd Chance*?

> (A very open question – anything could come up)
> Prompts – political views
>   – tolerance/assertiveness
>   – what they want to do with their lives

2. Have your attitudes towards/relationships with members of your family and friends changed in any way since *2nd Chance*?

3. Have your family's and friends' attitudes to you changed in any ways since *2nd Chance*?

Prompts – beneficial changes
        – problems created
---

4. Has your awareness of social problems facing different groups of people changed in any way since *2nd Chance*?

Prompts – women
        – black people
        – unemployed
        – employers
        – working class
(explore how they felt about these groups before *2nd Chance* and how they feel now)
---

5. Has your confidence changed in any ways since *2nd Chance*?

Prompts – do you have confidence to do different things?
        – do you feel more/less confident to speak up?

APPENDIX 10
Guidelines for Carrying out Interviews
(Issued to students on *Second Chance To Learn*)

Interviewing people is an important part of most research. You may need to interview a few individuals in great detail, interviews which might last an hour or more. Or you may wish to conduct a large number of quick interviews in order to accumulate a lot of statistical information. This might involve accosting strangers and perhaps asking them to answer a few short yes/no type questions. This needs to be approached with some caution, otherwise you may get more than you bargained for!

These two kinds of interview require different skills and will be dealt with separately below.

There are some preliminary points which are important to consider, whichever kind of interviewing you are doing.
1. Are you absolutely clear why you want certain information? If more than one of you will be conducting interviews, are you all clear that you are trying to do the same thing?
2. Exactly what questions will you ask?
3. Who will you ask and how will you contact them? Is your sample (the people you intend to ask) a *random sample* or a *selected sample?* You must be clear which. A random sample means picking people's names with a pin from a list of names. A selected sample means you decide in advance who it's to be e.g. *men, between the ages of 17 and 65, who have been unemployed for at least 6 months and who live in inner city areas.* That is a highly selected sample, but even then it leaves you with the problem of ensuring that you get an even spread of interviews over the whole inner city area, and the whole age range.

Guidelines for conducting a street survey, when a large number of interviewees are to be asked a few simple questions.
1. Make sure you have somewhere to keep all your bits of paper, a spare pen and something firm to write upon.
2. Smile!
3. Introduce yourself and your project (carry some written

identification) and explain clearly:
a) why you are seeking this information
b) how you intend to use it
c) that it will be anonymous

If you don't get this step right, you can forget the ones that follow as you won't get anyone agreeing to be interviewed!

Practice this with one another. Rehearse what you are going to say to a stranger. It's surprisingly difficult unless you have practice.

4. Decide in advance if you are planning to record the number of refusals – it's often important to do so. If you are, have a paper ready to record this.
5. Tell the interviewee how many questions you will be asking and how long it will take. Ask permission to write down the answers.
6. Ask each question slowly and clearly. If the interviewee looks puzzled, offer to repeat it. Don't rush, however nervous you may be.
7. Make sure you record each answer before you move on. Don't tell yourself you will be able to remember and will fill it in afterwards. You won't. Accuracy is essential, otherwise you are wasting your time (and everyone else's).
8. Avoid the kind of open questions which might lead to long rambling answers in a street interview. You won't be able to get the reply down properly, e.g. Don't ask *'What do you think about politics?'* Instead a list of short yes/no questions e.g. *'Did you vote in the last election? yes/no'. 'Do you intend to vote in the next one? yes/no,' 'Will you vote for the same party as you did before? yes/no.'*
9. Avoid linking two questions together or the resulting yes/no could apply to either and so will be useless to you when you come to tot up the answers later.
e.g. *'Do you know who your MP is and how to get in touch with him or her?'*
Ask these as two separate questions. More time consuming but, unless you do, the reply is useless.
10. Avoid asking too many questions. No one will stand around for more than a minute or two – 6 to 10 quick yes/no questions is reasonable. More often leads to trouble.
11. Thank your interviewee when you're finished. It's surprising

how often you'll forget as you rush to write down the final answers and try to avoid getting your papers blown away.

Conducting an in-depth interview

Before

1. Initial Contact. Write/phone explaining clearly and precisely who you are, what you are doing, why an interview with X would be useful, how long you expect it to take and, if you wish to use a cassette tape recorder, you should ask permission in advance. It is also a good idea to send your subject a set of questions in advance. This allows her/him to consider the answers; unless, of course, it is an important part of the research that you need spontaneous answers which haven't been carefully rehearsed.

2. Consider the benefits/disadvantages of using a tape recorder or making notes during the interview. Most unconfident interviewers prefer the former, but transcribing the tape afterwards is very time-consuming and if you don't need all that detail, then notes could be a much better answer. It really depends on a) how much detail you want and b) your confidence to interview and write notes simultaneously. How about taking a note-taker along with you?

3. If you plan to use a cassette recorder, practice first. Being shown which knobs to press just isn't enough. Set it up. Do a dummy run, so you get to know its problems.

4. Plan all your questions carefully in advance, and write them down. If more than one of you is going to ask questions, decide just who will ask what. If you don't do that, important things can get left out, or else one person takes over the whole thing and the others sit round feeling stupid.

During

1. When you arrive *smile*. However nervous you may feel, it's *your* job to set your interviewee at ease. Concentrate on that job and you will forget your own nerves.

2. Establish rapport – which means a bit of 'small talk' to put the interviewee at ease. Don't plunge in to the first question the moment you arrive. On the other hand don't spend half your valuable interview time getting friendly!

3. If you are going to use a tape recorder, set it up and *test it* before you begin, even if you tested it before you set off. Test it with your interviewee speaking so that you can check it is picking up her/his voice and your own. Many a blank or fuzzy tape has resulted from omitting this essential step. (See notes on **using a tape recorder** below).

4. Explain clearly what you are planning to do, e.g. how many questions you will be asking, what you are hoping to learn more about and why. If you haven't posted your interviewee a copy of the questions, this might be a good time to hand one over. Allow time for her/him to look through them.

5. Ask open-ended questions where possible (the very opposite of a street interview).

e.g. *'What do you think are the effects of unemployment upon family life?'*

Then, as your interviewee answers, follow up by individual prompt questions e.g. *'What leads you to believe that?'* or *'Have you any proof that that is happening?'* *'How often?'* etc.

The general idea is that once you open up a topic you follow up with very sharp questions designed to get your interviewee to be exact, otherwise you can be led into useless, vague waffle. Once you get back and try to put it down on paper, it adds up to nothing – a wasted interview.

6. Whilst asking these detailed follow-up questions (and never letting any important point slide vaguely by), you must take great care not to influence or lead. *It's very important neither to agree nor disagree.* Either of these may influence the following answers. Remember you have not come for a chat. Never say, *'Yes, I thought so as well,'* or *'Really, I didn't think that myself.'* Don't ask leading questions e.g. *'Don't you think that the Prime Minister was wrong to do X?'* It should always be, *'What do you think?'*

Even though you are not going to agree or disagree, that does not mean you have to remain silent. Instead you can say, *'Yes, I understand,'* if you do. If you are at all unsure, you should always check back that you have understood properly by saying something like this, *'Are you saying that ...?'*

or, *'I'm not sure if I've understood you correctly. Do you mean ...?'*

7. If the reply you get isn't very helpful e.g. *'Well, I'm not sure*

137

really,' probe further e.g. *'Have you ever considered this, or talked about it with anyone?'* Sometimes you will still get nowhere, but it's amazing how a gentle prod sometimes produces whole new trains of thought. Sometimes *'Well, I'm not sure really,'* means, *'I don't really understand what it is you are wanting,'* and so simply by rephrasing your question you can produce results. In probing it is useful to say something like, *'That's interesting. Tell me more about it.'*

8. Sometimes probing or following up particular leads means you have to change the order of your questions. Don't be afraid to, if it seems useful. But if you do have to, check very carefully before you leave that you have not forgotten to ask some of your questions. This happens quite often.

9. If you are making notes on the reply rather than using a tape, accuracy is difficult to achieve but obviously very important. Always

    a) ask permission to make notes

    b) ask questions one at a time – don't link ideas up, it gets confusing

    c) listen carefully (don't write yet)

    d) then check out your intended notes for accuracy e.g. *'So if I write down . . would that be a fair summary of what you've just said?'*

    e) then write it down quickly but fully

    f) be sure to ask her/him to repeat anything you didn't fully hear or understand.

10. If your interviewee is wandering off into an irrelevant discussion, be direct, tackle it. You cannot afford to waste your own or your interviewee's time. *'I'd like to move on to look at ...'* or *'Although I find that very interesting, I'm afraid we can't spend any longer on that point . . .'* should tactfully move things on.

11. Look back over your list of questions to make sure you haven't forgotten any.

12. Remember to thank the person for her/his time.

After

1. If you made notes during the interview, it is essential to get the notes written up immediately, before you lose track of what was said. Do it the same day. If you are conducting more than one interview in a day, try to write up one before conducting the second,

otherwise you may end up confusing the two.

2. If you use a tape, you will need to transcribe it as soon as possible. Though speed is less essential than in a note-taking interview, it is still important not to delay, as it gets increasingly difficult to remember the details with every day that passes. This makes an already difficult task much harder.

Transcribing a tape is a hard and tedious task. Try doing it with someone else. Following these steps may help:

a) Listen to the tape right through. Don't make detailed notes, but just jot down the main points which emerge – a couple of words for each.

These will form headings.

b) Look at your headings and think back to what you were trying to get out of the interview. That will help you decide how much detail you will need to get down under each heading. The headings will hopefully be very closely linked to your questions though there may be several additional ones.

c) Listen again. Get down more detail this time – stopping the tape as often as necessary. But *don't* attempt to write down every word spoken. You have to be very selective, and you need to summarise what your interviewee was saying.

d) If necessary, listen again to perhaps add some quotations if they would be of use. Finally write it all out clearly. To do this you may want to simply follow the order of your notes from the tape. If so, be sure to indicate your questions and, if you asked extra questions, you may need to write these in.

A Question/Answer format can be easier to read and to write than a mass of dense print.

You may think it better to group certain ideas together because they are linked (rather like you do when you arrange ideas for an essay). This may mean quite a lot of rearranging of your original summary of the interview.

e) Having produced the final summary, it is a good idea to listen back over the tape once more to check you haven't missed out anything important or, more likely, altered it all slightly so it says what you *wanted* to hear rather than what you *did* hear!

Of course that is a very thorough approach. You need to consider whether such detail is necessary. But if it isn't, do you really need that tape recorder?

Using a Tape Recorder

1. Choose a room which is fairly quiet. Some background noise adds atmosphere (e.g. clocks, moderate street noise) while other sounds interrupt the flow (e.g. doors banging, TVs, telephone, gas fires roaring). Street noise can be reduced by simply drawing the curtains or choosing a room at the back of the house. Avoid sparsely furnished rooms as these create echoes.

2. Check out the recorder before beginning. Make sure it is recording by doing a test recording. Recite into the microphone a few words. Play it back then adjust the volume if necessary.

3. Place the tape recorder on a chair rather than on the table on which you will be placing the microphone. The microphone should be placed approximately half way between yourself and the subject, slightly to one side to avoid the subject staring at the microphone. Ensure that the machine is as far away from the microphone as is practicable because this avoids picking up motor noise and vibrations from the recorder. Also try to cushion the microphone with a table cloth, or even newspapers, to stop sound reflection from the table.

Adjust the sound level by asking the subject to recite or read something and do the same for yourself. Make sure you are getting a good response according to the distance of each person from the mike by checking the needle on the sound meter if there is one. (The needle should move up to the red mark and back again to the rising and falling of sounds.)

On most machines the sound level is controlled by the A.L.C. device which prevents over-recording. However, this can be over-ridden by manual controls.

N.B. A.L.C. Means automatic level control.

APPENDIX 11
A Case Study

From **J. Edwards,** *Working Class Adult Education in Liverpool: A Radical Approach.* 1986, Manchester Monographs.

Dot is thirty-two, married and has two sons aged seven and five. As well as running her home, she works part-time in a shop. What brought her to *Second Chance?* She loved her primary school, where she felt she was well taught. It was a different story when she moved into the senior part of the same school.

'It was an old school. You know, one typewriter and one sewing machine between six classes.'

Everything changed. After being 'stretched' in primary school:

'It was a case of, "There's no need to do anything because when you reach fifteen you're going to leave school and get a job. There's no need to bother about education". No one pushed us. Everyone seemed to be messing around and no one took any notice of it. At that time I still did want education, and I remember then at eleven, I still wanted to learn, but what the teacher was trying to give us was no good.'

She still feels bitter today that she never had the opportunity to go on learning once she got into secondary school.

Dot had always enjoyed learning, both in her primary school and then in her first job. But, like so many women, she had always been thwarted and never achieved all she felt she could and wanted to. After the birth of her first child, she intended to begin a new career – doing whatever courses might be required. Then her mother, who was to mind that child, had a stroke. Once again she was stopped. For the next seven years she waited, always intending to come back. But by the time her second child had entered school, her confidence had dropped so low that she couldn't contemplate either a career or any kind of formal education, especially with exams. *Second Chance* appeared to be just right: easy, informal, no exams, precisely what she needed in order to begin again.

It was the easy, informal approach which attracted her rather than the content of the course. All she knew was she wanted something academic (not a leisure class) but not too frightening. Even so it took courage. She tore up her first application form and was terrified of the interview, and very anxious about her first day.

Dot had been active in a local voluntary project sponsored by the *Save the Children Fund* for two years and soon after she began attending *Second Chance to Learn* she became chairperson of this group. She attributes her confidence to allow herself to be nominated as chairperson (and the skills she has developed in chairing) partly to *Second Chance to Learn* where, in tutorials, she was helped to organise her work as chairperson. In discussion groups she learned about chairing groups effectively. In seminars she acquired valuable information, especially about how the local City Council works. Being able to pass on that information in meetings of her committee, especially finding she knew things which others in full-time employment did not know, has given her a lot of confidence.

> *'When I voiced my opinion and someone was saying, "Is that right?" I just couldn't believe it. These people doing those big jobs didn't know.'*

Although initially she was not particularly attracted to the content of the course, she found she enjoyed it all, even those parts she did not expect to enjoy. The main thing that changed was her confidence, both in herself and in her ability to study.

> *'I'm on the road now and there's no way I'll go back to the way I was before.'*

Second Chance changed her attitude to those in authority – teachers, doctors etc. Dot describes how, directly as a result of her developing confidence, she went up to school to discuss her son's difficulties.

> *'With going on Second Chance, I went up to school to sort it out and ask them what they are teaching and tell them I thought he had potential.'*

She felt able to query her mother's medical treatment for the first time ever and, as a result, prevented a serious illness. How did this confidence come about?

> *'With the tutors being so friendly, getting to know them, I began to think, "Well, they're normal, so probably teachers in this (her son's) school are normal. They're not so big and not so*

alienated." By the confidence from here you can challenge these people. Not being nasty. Just ask about things, rather than just moan about them behind their backs and never even do anything about it. If I want to find something out now, I'd just go and ask them about it. Whether they think I'm stupid or not, I'll just ask.'

Her confidence and enthusiasm affected others. A friend, very sceptical of Dot's new interest in education, has been 'converted' and is herself applying for a course.

'She doesn't think it's so stupid any more. Considering her attitude before, she was the sort of person who'd say, "Oh I'm all right. I don't need it." Seeing me change, she's changed and she's going to do a course.'

She can now hold her own in conversations, at home and with men.

'I feel as though I don't want to sit there and be quiet any more. Now, if I felt as though I disagreed with them, I would openly say I disagreed and why I disagreed. I didn't before. I used to think, "How come they know all this and I don't? Where have I missed out?" Now I feel I know something about that.'

She finds men treating her differently now, with more respect. This confidence has come about mainly because she feels she knows something about the topics her husband and his friends discuss, or information needed by her committee. It also comes from the fact that her writing has improved greatly. When she began *Second Chance to Learn* one of her main aims was to get better at writing.

'I really have improved my writing. On my committee I produced the notes. It took me three days, but it was typed and passed round everyone, and I felt pleased with it.'

She's learned how to study, too.

'Study skills – I keep having to go back to them because that's my main problem. I know how to do them now, so it's up to me to do it.'

Although her political views have not changed, Dot has become more enquiring.

'I used to vote . . . before because it was a thing that went from one family to another. I didn't think about it; just did it. I would

question now some of their opinions about things. I'd think, "Couldn't they do this or that?" whereas before I just went in and signed a cross.'

Her experience of *Second Chance* has also affected her family. Her young children, seeing her studying, want to sit down and write things themselves. They ask her lots more questions and she feels able either to answer them or knows how to find things out to give them an answer. She has passed on her new-found knowledge to her children.

'And if they ask something I don't really know about, now I'd get a book and read up on it and explain to them and then tell them why, and where I got the book from, so they'll do that for themselves now. Whereas when I was little, I'd ask my mum and she'd say, "Oh, I don't know," and that was it.'

Dot's horizons have completely changed during her time on *Second Chance to Learn*. Although she's not certain of her goal, having waited seven years for the opportunity, she feels nothing will stop her now.

'At the moment I'm not planning beyond the next twelve months. Then there'll be far more doors open and I'll take it one step at a time.'

The only problem she experienced was that when she was offered a place, her husband could not understand why she wanted a course like *Second Chance* and would have felt much happier if she'd just gone and done maths and book-keeping in an evening class. He could not see why she wanted the challenge of something much bigger. He felt resentful of his wife's new confidence and self-assertion in discussions with his friends and other men. Some months after leaving *Second Chance*, Dot separated from her husband. She had wanted to do this many times during preceding years but lacked the confidence in her ability to go it alone. They are now divorced and she says she is happily rebuilding her life.

Dot's story, her school experiences, her reasons for enrolling and the changes which occurred during her year on *Second Chance*, echo the experiences of many students.

APPENDIX 12
Teaching Evaluation Checklist 1

(to be used when colleagues observe one another)

SESSION AND DATE ....TEACHER................................

OBSERVER...

(These 10 headings are spread out over a double-sided sheet to allow space for comments to be written)

1. AIMS: are they clearly stated and preferably displayed?

2. CONTEXT: does the introduction make clear the reason for this session and how it relates to the course?

3. CONTENT: is it clearly thought out and the right amount?

4. STUDENT INVOLVEMENT: remembering that we learn most effectively through doing, is there an active role for students; how much of the time are they simply listening or watching?

5. PRACTICAL WORK: are all tasks clearly explained and preferably written up?

6. PREPARATORY MATERIAL: does the material prepare students for the session and is it appropriate?

7. AIDS AND RESOURCES: what is used other than chalk and the human voice; is it effective?

8. METHODS: what methods are used and for how long; is there variety or is one method used throughout; are methods appropriate?

9. ATMOSPHERE: conducive to learning and relaxed . . . or what?

10. IMPROVEMENTS: how could it have been done better: different method; different lay-out; better preparation?

APPENDIX 13
Teaching Evaluation Checklist II

(adapted from a checklist used on the City and Guilds 7307 teacher training course at Oldham College, with thanks to Gordon Hall)

	RELATIONSHIPS	
12. Attitude of the Teacher		Teacher adopts a friendly and co-operative attitude towards the students. S/he is encouraging and helpful. The teacher is not autocratic.
13. Participation		The teacher encourages and initiates student participation.
14. Motivation		The teacher attempts to motivate the students.

	QUESTIONING	
15. Questioning Technique		The teacher uses questions for confirmation of learning.
16. Question Construction		The teacher phrases questions in a form which makes the meaning clear. Questions are appropriate to the students' level of knowledge.

	ASSESSING	
17. Testing		The teacher devises appropriate ways of testing what the students have learned – either by written, verbal or practical test.
18. Evaluating		The teacher uses appropriate written or verbal questions to evaluate the lesson.

PRESENTATION	1. Aims and objectives	It is made clear to the students what the teacher intends to do.
	2. Lesson Plan	A lesson plan has been prepared showing teaching method and student activity.
	3. Environment	The learning environment is arranged to optimise the smooth execution of the lesson.
	4. Stimulus	A variety of verbal and non-verbal techniques are used to maintain an alert interest by the students in the subject or skill.
PREPARATION	5. Communication	Two way communication is maintained. Communication from the teacher involves speech, body language, eye-contact, supporting media and demonstration.
	6. Knowledge of Subject	The teacher demonstrates knowledge and skill in her/his subject appropriate to the students' requirements.
	7. Lesson	The lesson moves forward at a pace suited to student ability. The planned strategy is implemented.
	8. Learning Aids	Aids are competently used and appropriate to the lesson.
	9. Lesson Timing	The lesson is accurately timed.
	10. Variation of activity	The teacher varies activity in the lesson to maintain attention.
	11. Personal Characteristics	The voice is well modulated with clear diction. Volume and projection of the voice are adequate; the teacher demonstrates competent articulation: no personal distracting mannerisms are evident.

APPENDIX 14
Session Evaluation Sheet

Date: ....Title of session: ....

Time: ....Name of Teacher: ....

Rating

(not useful)	1	2	3	4	5	(very useful)
(not enjoyable)	1	2	3	4	5	(very enjoyable)

Comments

Recommended Changes

Copies of this sheet could be distributed at the end of sessions and should be collected in immediately.

A series of these could be typed together on one or more sheets of paper forming a booklet. Students could then complete the evaluation sheet at the end of each lesson but retain the booklet. At the end of the course or unit, completed booklets could be handed in, allowing the evaluator to trace each person's developing reactions to the course. If such a booklet is provided, space could be made for students to evaluate the course (or unit) in its entirety by, for example, altering the last evaluation sheet as follows.

Title of course/unit: ....

Rating

(not useful)	1	2	3	4	5	(very useful)
(not enjoyable)	1	2	3	4	5	(very enjoyable)

Comments on the course

Recommended Changes

APPENDIX 15

Methods of Class Evaluation

(Workers' Educational Association, 1985)

Method	Who is the evaluation for?	Strengths	Weaknesses
1. **A written class secretary's report**	Branch (Newsletter?) District T/O (Tutor Organiser). Should be filled in after class discussion.	Involves Class Secretary in a voluntary-led, positive form of feedback. Enhances role of Class Secretary. Raises specific issues. Identifies problems. Complements tutor's report. Improves links between course and Branch. A formal record on paper. Need good proforma.	As good as the form. May not be representative. Too late to deal with problems. Onerous burden on Class Secretary? How objective can it be?
2. **A verbal report by a class secretary** to a Branch committee	Branch committee. Information can be collected and passed to T/O and District.	Immediate. Positive feedback can be clarified and discussed. May allow for greater honesty through informality. May lead to improvements later in same course. Involves Class Secretary at Branch level.	Very personal view. Often little preparation. Can a large Branch process a lot of verbal reports?
3. **Tutor's self-evaluation**, using a check list	Tutor. Possible to discuss with T/O and/or class	Increases self-awareness. Aids reflection and can stimulate change. Creates expectation that evaluation should be ongoing process. Encourages tutor to think about teaching methods and WEA aims as well as the subject. Quality of checklist important.	Open to self-deception! Most useful in context of tutor training.
4. **Tutor's Report Form** sent to Branch or District	District and T/Os. Copy could be sent on from District to Branch.	Commits tutor to review course. Gives opportunity for tutor to criticise Branch when necessary. Complements Class Secretary's report. Available for future reference.	Can be anodyne. Tutors may not admit problems. Comes at the end of a course, therefore too late for changes.
5. **Individual Questionnaires for students**	Branch and T/O. Depends on who initiates it – Branch, FT Staff or Tutor.	Opportunity for all students to participate. Allows specific issues to be surveyed. For publicity. May influence tutors' approach.	Compilation important. May alienate tutor. Problems of coping with analysis.

Method	Used by	Advantages	Problems
6. **Class Log.** A report of each week's session, written by members of the class in turn in a common book. Can include evaluation of the course.	Class. Tutor. Branch. Posterity via publication.	Involves students in producing a written report. Provides ongoing review of course. Encourages student skills and cooperative learning. Gives continuity from year to year.	Time consuming. Is it a report or an evaluation? Could be threatening to some students.
7. **Tutor-led discussion on progress.** The tutor might ask: "How are we progressing through the syllabus?" "What have we got out of today's class?" "Where do we go from here?"	Class and Tutor	Class involvement. Ongoing evaluation of syllabus and course progress. Reinforcement of knowledge. Reflection on what has been learned.	Tutor may be too intrusive. May be too time consuming. Could be dominated by a minority. An unwillingness to criticise.
8. **Class meeting.** The class meets regularly during the course, chaired by a member of the class, to discuss the progress of the class – the tutor is involved but does not run the meeting (often used on longer and more intensive courses).	Class and Tutor	Democratic control particularly useful in longer courses. Strong student involvement. Development of ideas.	Could be time-consuming. Could lead to class being self-congratulatory.
9. **Coffee-break evaluation**	Tutor, Class, Branch	Informal student participation. Students relaxed not threatened. Experienced can support new students. On the spot improvements can be made.	Unstructured. Lack of feedback. Danger of gossip. Student cliques and tutor, or individual student alienation.
10. Other: (a) **Visit by FT staff,** (b) **Final meeting discussion of course,** (c) **Commitment of class,** (through attendance etc).	Branch and District. Class and Tutor	(a) Introduces FT (full time) Staff to students. (b) Highlights training needs. (c) Student involvement.	(a) Time-consuming, inhibiting to students. (b) Too late. Students may be inhibited.

Which method(s) are best? Depends on Branch/District structure. All the methods currently used, could be improved. 1, 2, 3 and 7 are of most use to those doing them. 2, 3 and 7 were most favoured.

149

APPENDIX 16
Evaluation Training
Pre-Training Questionnaire for Participants I

In order to ensure that we get the maximum benefit from the **Initial Training Session,** will you please answer the following questions and bring the sheets with you to the first session. Please try to find time to talk to your fellow course team members about these questions before the meeting, as their opinions and ideas are just as important as yours. You can complete separate sheets or do a joint sheet if preferred.

N.B. All your replies will be treated confidentially and nothing will be discussed or reported outside of the training sessions without the agreement of participants.

Name(s)

1. What questions would you like to have answered about the proposed evaluation?

2. What problems do you anticipate which need our consideration, and what worries do you have about the proposed evaluation?

3. Are there any other issues which you feel should be addressed during the training sessions?

4. Do you have any previous experience of carrying out evaluation procedures?

5. Do you have any thoughts about other aspects of training which would benefit you?

APPENDIX 17
Evaluation Training
Pre-Training Questionnaire for Participants II

This or a similar set of questions can be circulated to anyone intending to attend an evaluation training session. They are of greater value if sent out a week or more in advance. But they can be useful if distributed on the day of the training event. Small groups can talk together and pool ideas. This activity is especially useful at the start of a training session.

Please complete these questions before attending the Evaluation Training Day, as far as you are able to:

1. What are the stated aims/goals for the project or scheme you are working with? *(You may never have seen these. If not, can you try to get hold of them.)*

2. What do you personally believe your project or scheme should be trying to achieve? *(This list may be identical to your answer to question (1) or could bear little resemblance.)*

3. What steps, if any, do you take to communicate your goals to your students/clients/users?

4. What steps, if any, do you take to assess whether these goals are being met? *(List anything you may have undertaken e.g. questionnaires, discussions, work reports etc. Say how often these are used.)*

5. What steps, if any, do you take to follow up your students/clients/users and find out how valuable your service is in the long term?

6. In what ways do you attempt to assess your own effectiveness as a worker?

7. To what extent do your students/users/clients have an opportunity to assess *your* work and that of the project as a whole?

8. What do you anticipate as the greatest obstacles to a thorough evaluation of your project/work?

9. What do you anticipate would be the benefits of an evaluation of your project/work?

APPENDIX 18
Evaluation Training
Monitoring and Evaluation – Workshop I

(by courtesy of **Elizabeth Whale, Birmingham Quality Development Unit)**

A useful activity at the start of a training event. The sheets can be distributed in advance, or at the time of the event. Groups can share experiences and identify common issues.

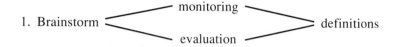

1. Brainstorm — monitoring / evaluation — definitions

2. Why do you want to be involved in evaluation now?

3. What monitoring and evaluation activity have you been involved in in the past?

4. Who directed that activity?

5. Who else was involved?

6. What was your role in it?

7. What areas of the curriculum were being investigated?

8. Who decided that?

9. What sort of methods were used?

10. Who decided on those?

11. How did colleagues/students feel about it?

12. Who had access to the information collected?

13. How was it recorded? ·

14. How was it reported back to staff/students?

15. How was it helpful/unhelpful?

16. What changed as a result?

APPENDIX 19
Evaluation Training
Questions for Use at the Start of a Workshop

A set of questions which can be used as a starter activity at the beginning of an evaluation training event.

1a. How do you currently evaluate the quality of your services/ courses/ individual teachers/ tutors/ yourself?

1b. What problems have you encountered in attempting evaluation?

2. Is what you do sufficient? If not, what ideas do you have to extend evaluation?

3a. Are your students involved in evaluating their courses/ tutors/ services?

3b. Could they be?

3c. What problems do you anticipate?

4. Do you/others need further training to improve the quality of evaluation? If so, what?

5. What practical steps do you intend to take now?

APPENDIX 20
Evaluation Training
Questions for Use in a Workshop

*Questions such as these can be useful during an evaluation training event. If, for example, you are organising an initial one day event, these questions can be effective if used towards the end of the day. Participants can thus begin to plan. They would normally return to their work places, discuss these questions with colleagues, then set themselves specific targets with dates for commencement and completion (**Appendix 4** can be useful for setting targets.)*

It can be useful to organise a further training session and to recall participants to discover what progress they are making, what problems they are encountering, and their emerging training needs.

During this session try to get something concrete begun.

1. How will you ascertain the aims (e.g. of your scheme, of your tutors, the organisers, the students)? Who will you ask? Will you discuss it as a group, or with individuals? Who'll do the asking, and who'll draw up the answers into some statement?

2. What do you want to find out? (prioritize these as you will discover a small piece of evaluation takes time).

3. Who will you want to ask questions of?

4. What methods might you use? e.g.
   - questionnaires
   - in-depth interview with individuals
   - group interviewing
   - observation of work
   - filling in time sheets
   - filling in record sheets
   - others

5. How will you use your findings? Who will see them?

6. How will you allay anxieties and overcome reluctance?

7. How can evaluation become part of your way of working?